Gifted by Otherness

GIFTED BY
OTHERNESS

GAY AND LESBIAN CHRISTIANS IN THE CHURCH

L. WILLIAM COUNTRYMAN

and

M. R. RITLEY

MOREHOUSE PUBLISHING

To Malcolm Boyd,
poet, priest, and prophet,
and
to all those other gay and lesbian pioneers
who have said yes to God's call

Morehouse Publishing
P.O. Box 1321
Harrisburg, PA 17105

Morehouse Publishing is a division of The Morehouse Group.

Cover design by Tom Castanzo

Library of Congress Cataloging-in-Publication Data
Countryman, Louis William, 1941-
   Gifted by otherness : gay and lesbian Christians in the church / L. William Countryman and M. R. Ritley.
     p. cm.
   Includes bibliographical references.
   ISBN 0-8192-1886-3 (alk. paper)
       1. Christian gays—Religious life. 2. Homosexuality—Religious aspects—Christianity. I. Ritley, M. R. II. Title.

BV4596.G38 C68 2001
261.8'35766—dc21   00-067899

Printed in the United States of America
01 02 03 04 05 06 07 08 09   10 9 8 7 6 5 4 3 2 1

CONTENTS

ACKNOWLEDGMENTS

The material in this book has gone through a great many developments as we presented it in workshops, taught it in classes, and discussed it over the last five years. We owe many thanks to The Church Divinity School of the Pacific, Berkeley, California, where we have taught classes on gay spirituality, and to the students whose thoughtful and lively responses added so much to our understanding. Special acknowledgments go to the Sorrento Centre, British Columbia, where we presented the material in this book during a week-long workshop in July, 1998. The warm and supportive help of the staff, especially Marks MacAvity and Wayne McNamara, added greatly to the week, and no acknowledgments would be complete without a special bow to Eddie Nishida, whose tapes of the workshop were an indispensable help in getting this book on paper.

— L. W. C. and M. R. R.

The friends to whom I owe particular thanks for conversations about these issues are too numerous to list in full, but I must at least mention Bill Doubleday, Chris Eastoe, Richard Hardy, Joseph Lane, Joe McInerney, Jim Newman, Marni Schneider, Rob Stiefel—and, not least, my partner Jon Vieira. Tom Schultz, OHC, my spiritual advisor for some years now, has had an important, if indirect, influence on the work, as he continually presses me on the importance of offering hope in a difficult world.

   I owe thanks to The Church Divinity School of the Pacific for sabbatical time in the fall of 2000, during which this project came to completion, and to the Conant Fund for a challenge grant that helped me keep this particular sabbatical free for writing and thinking.

— L. W. C.

Many friends and colleagues have helped me develop these ideas and encouraged me to get them on paper, but any list would be headed by Malcolm Boyd, who has been friend, parish priest, and fellow traveler on the pilgrimage of gay spirituality, and Marilyn McCord Adams, who has not only kept me thinking, but has helped me keep my faith and humor alive.

The Church Divinity School of the Pacific's Doctor of Ministry program, headed by Dr. Alda Marsh Morgan, has been an indispensable piece of this book's genesis. Most of my chapters were written as part of the program, with the lively encouragement and always helpful criticism of my fellow students Kate Campbell, Daniel Cho, Ruth Fiscella, Vann Knight, Toni Longo, and Glenna Shepherd, and my project committee Don Compier, Russell Moy, and (of course!) Bill Countryman.

Finally, I owe an enormous debt of gratitude to Rick Fabian and Donald Schell, rectors of St. Gregory of Nyssa Episcopal Church, San Francisco, and to the staff, vestry, and people of that congregation. It says a great deal about their generosity of spirit that they not only encouraged and believed in me, but provided me with both the time and financial support necessary to complete this project.

– M. R. R.

Oakland, California
Feast of Aelred of Rievaulx, 2001

WHOSE PROBLEM ARE WE?

A Question of Perception

M. R.: Several years ago, a friend who knows my sense of humor very well sent me a card for no occasion in particular, just on the assumption that *(a)* I would get a good laugh out of it, and *(b)* I probably needed one. The front was designed to look like one of those egregious tabloids that I am unable to keep from picking up in the checkout line. In this case, instead of "Mom, 7, Gives Birth to Elvis-Lookalike Space Alien," the headline shrieked "Shocking Secrets of . . . . THE GAY LIFESTYLE!" It was illustrated with a 1950s couple, eyes wide in horror, mouths agape. The picture had probably come from a movie poster for a grade-B horror flick.

Beneath the scandalized couple, smaller headlines screamed:

"SEE THEM . . . mow the lawn!

"HEAR THEM . . . order Chinese take-out!

"WATCH THEM . . . do the laundry!"

Inside, my friend had written, "The truth is out at last! I always wondered why, if my life is such a scandal, it's so *dull*? Happy Monday, Vicki."

And there it is in a nutshell, I thought: Vicki, a longtime vestry member in her parish, lay eucharistic minister, former youth group leader, and regular volunteer at a parish-run feeding program, knows perfectly well that her picture of her life as a lesbian Christian and her church's picture are light-years apart. She knows, moreover, which picture is true, though she will probably never convince her co-parishioners, much less her church. Like most of us who know ourselves to be gay, she has had to find her way to a spiritual center from which to define her own life and faith, refusing the definitions that the straight majority confidently uses to describe her. The reality of this is not nearly as humorous as the card suggests, but those who have survived several decades of church life know that sometimes only humor keeps them from becoming as aberrant as their coreligionists frequently tell them they are.

In fact, it is always astonishing to discover how many healthy and self-affirming gay women and men are to be found in the churches, and how much humor and courage they bring to the task of being Christians in a world that views Christians with suspicion and to the task of being gay in Christian churches that view being gay with condemnation, fear, or anger. Somehow, they have managed to remain faithful Christians, genuinely devoted to their various churches, trying to live out both the gospel imperative and the truth of their own lives.

But there are so few compared to the larger number of gay men and lesbians who either become refugees from churches that will not accept them or remain in their communities, hidden and silent, either fearful of being known for who they are or brainwashed into believing that the church is right in condemning them in the first place.

Redefining the "Problem" of Gay and Lesbian Christians

It is not that the church ignores the question of how to deal with gay and lesbian members: far from it. Like other minority groups, LesBiGay Christians have been part of the larger liberation movements that, since the early sixties, have rejected the majority's assumptions and definitions, challenged both the morality and truthfulness of those definitions, and insisted on the right of self-definition.

To many people, gay and straight alike, it seems that little else has taken center stage at church conventions, councils, or synods in the last decade, so that for many genuinely engaged gay and lesbian Christians, these meetings have become what one gay man, with more imagination than delicacy, called the "annual faggot-flaying." The difficulty is that this attention is overwhelmingly focused on what others see as the "problem" of gay and lesbian Christians, rather than the problem that heterosexual Christians pose to us. This latter is far more severe a problem, given the damage it inflicts on gay and lesbian lives, or encourages others to inflict.

Over the past few years, in fact, the discussion has definitely escalated, and in proportion to its escalation, it has become more and more charged with animosity. Many perfectly ordinary gay and lesbian Christians discover, to their amazement, that they are apparently the greatest threat to Christianity since the Emperor Nero. Moreover, the very fact that they are asking the church to bless same-gender marriages as it does cross-gender marriages is somehow seen as proof of how dire a threat they are to marriage and family.

In the midst of this discussion, debate, and ever-more-desperate attempt for one side or another to achieve an absolute victory (one of the most aberrant of all twentieth-century obsessions, by the way), the genuine pastoral and emotional needs of gay and lesbian Christians are simply ignored, while one more discussion, dialogue, or debate takes place. These needs—and the freight of human pain and human need they represent—continue unabated while the church decides what to do about the problem. Clearly, the divided church itself is in no position to offer either moral or spiritual leadership here, or at least in any way timely enough to matter to a great many gay and lesbian Christians whose pain, confusion, and anger can certainly not be put on hold while the discussion goes on.

To be fair, the church has its own troubles over the question of sexuality, gay or otherwise. Sincere Christians are committed to remaining at the discussion table, unwilling to break fellowship with other Christians, however hotly they disagree. As a Christian, I appreciate their willingness to continue the dialogue; as a gay woman, I deplore this substitution of discussion for ministry, particularly when the real-life needs of men and women are flagrantly ignored.

There lies the central difficulty, it seems: one community waiting while another (which has too often shown itself to be ignorant or ill-informed at best and hostile at worst) decides its fate and meaning. Whatever the dominant community's answer is, the process in itself is both unacceptable and unchristian. It is the right of a community to define itself, a lesson that the church is only slowly learning in the cases of other minority groups and that it has as yet failed to apply to the gay and lesbian Christians in its midst.

Dealing with the "problem," then, is actually a matter of devising ways in which the gay and lesbian Christian community can begin a deeper process of self-definition, placing itself not only in the community-at-large, but specifically defining its role in the church—and doing it, moreover, not simply in the church's terms, but in terms that it has already redefined in the light of its own experience. This is a central task of what gay and lesbian Christians must undertake on their own behalf. Moreover, it must rest solidly on the gay-lesbian community's refusal to be defined as the problem: there is clearly a problem, but it is a problem of attitude on the heterosexual community's part, and one of the first steps in healthy gay and lesbian self-definition is the rejection of the role of "problem" and the refusal to be punished for the heterosexual community's failure to deal with its own problem.

What does it look like when gay men and women appropriate and interpret the biblical story, act out the gospel message, and draw on their own cultures (including gay humor) to give them color, meaning, and texture? This is, I believe, a task that must be done *by* gay men and women as well as *with* gay men and women, not something the church does *for* gay men and women. This kind of appropriation has been a major strength to other minority groups, notably the African American community and third-world Christians. Gays and lesbians must consciously frame such a spiritual foundation.

Whether the church decides at length that LesBiGay people should be here—lay, ordained, single or coupled—we already *are* here, and what is needed is not simply and passively asking for the church's acceptance, but creating a gay spiritual understructure powerful enough to reshape the very terms in which the church perceives and understands us. Such a reversal is not easily achieved, either in an individual's life or in the awareness of a larger community. Hence, the emphasis of this book: a proactive stance, not a mere rebuttal of the church's teaching, but a means of reeducating both the gay and straight communities.

A Peculiar Kind of Ministry

Gay men and lesbians have an astonishing degree of tenacity: they must, just to persist in being faithful to themselves in a world that has shown itself to be hostile, untrustworthy, and dangerous. Their continuing presence in the church century after century is a fairly impressive feat in and of itself. Like other oppressed communities, the LesBiGay world has been shaped by the need to "hide in plain sight." To this end, it has developed its own language—especially words and phrases used only in gay settings and by gay people—particular styles of dress, gestures, and especially a certain kind of humor that have kept gay people's spirit, dignity, and self-determination alive.

Oddly enough, in a church increasingly aware of the need for sensitivity to the cultural contexts of other groups it seeks to minister to, there is a peculiar blindness to gay cultural contexts, as if they had neither legitimacy nor respectability, and could therefore safely be ignored while a version of Christianity approved by the majority was superimposed on this minority. Such a strategy in dealing with any other minority would be horrifying to mainstream churches nowadays, a legacy of nineteenth-century cultural imperialism. It may take a significant amount of education to convince the churches that, just as they should not treat Asians, Africans, or Native Americans as defective Europeans, neither should they pretend that gay and lesbian Christians are defective heterosexuals.

What does it mean, what does it look like, when gay and lesbian Christians can come to understand themselves as God's gay people, exploring God's love and wisdom in gay lives, gay relationships, and gay communities? Granted, this is a peculiar ministry when viewed by many straight Christians, but most cultures are strange when viewed by ethnocentric outsiders.

Caught in the Middle

Bill: Lesbian and gay Christians often find that we are trying to explain ourselves to two different and mutually hostile audiences. On one side, the gay-lesbian community is often deeply suspicious of anybody connected with Christianity. Many of us, individually and as a group, have excellent reason for such feelings, having been treated very harshly and dismissively by churches. Some people who claim to speak for Christianity really do have an anti-gay agenda, and they sometimes take an active political role in trying to keep gay and lesbian people from sharing the rights that other citizens of modern democracies take for granted—the right to freedom of speech, for example, the right to basic security in habitation and employment, and the right to form legally recognized families. Given all this, many gay men and lesbians have a hard time understanding why we would still be engaged with the Christian faith.

The churches, on the other hand, even when they are not actively hostile to us, often seem to wish that we would go away or at least disappear quietly into the woodwork. They wonder why we cannot leave well enough alone and just be grateful that we're no longer being denounced, expelled, or even executed. A good many of our heterosexual co-religionists think of us as creating a problem by our presence. We belong to the ranks of the "tolerated," and the classic fantasy of toleration is that the tolerated ought to be so grateful for that status that they meekly submit to whatever lingering indignities may go with it. Churches, then—with some happy exceptions—wonder why we have to be gay at all; or, if it's really unavoidable, why we have to *talk* about it.

One may well wonder why we put up with living in this particular spot, under suspicion from both the communities that we identify with. At bottom, I think it's a matter of congruence; our sexuality and our faith actually do go together. Whatever the church may say, we have found in our gayness something that connects us with ourselves and with God. Churches may have given Christian faith a bad name in our community, but our own experience of that faith has helped us understand and rejoice in who we are. God has enriched us in creating us as the lesbian and gay people we are.

In a corresponding way, our experience as gay men and lesbians enables us to see our Christian faith with new eyes. Some of the things we were told about Christianity turn out to have been wrong and harmful; other things turn out to be amazingly and unexpectedly life-giving. Our sexual orientation—or rather our whole life experience, which includes our sexual orientation—has actually been the occasion of our faith coming awake and giving us life. We bring to the churches, then, a perspective that renews and revives the central message of the gospel, the good news that forms the foundation for everything that is legitimately Christian.

Each aspect of our identity as lesbian and gay Christians offers gifts to the other. And each side needs the gifts that the other side brings. We persist in living on this awkward boundary not out of some inability to give up childhood religious training, not out of some reluctance to be fully gay or fully Christian, but out of a sense that this is the richest place we could possibly live. That doesn't mean, of course, that it is free from problems. There are moments for all of us, I suspect, when we would really like to belong simply to one community or the other—but the losses would be too great.

The Vocation of Being Caught in the Middle

From the perspective of Christian faith, this awkward business of living on the boundary looks very much like vocation—a call from God. When you answer such a call, you discover the meaning of your life. God has drawn us to this difficult place in order to reveal God's grace to us and in us and through us. The boundary where we're living, however inconvenient, is a place rich in spiritual discovery—which means, of course, that it is also largely uncharted territory. No ready-made tradition tells us how to be gay and lesbian Christians. This is a vocation God has created in our own time to bring about a new enrichment of the gospel.

Not that there haven't been gay men and lesbians in the church from the very beginning. Undoubtedly there have been, even though they're largely invisible in the record. A generation ago, churches depended heavily on closeted gays to fill the ranks of clergy. They still do, in those places and denominations where it isn't safe to come out of the closet. The difference today is not that lesbians and gay men are part of the church, but that we are *open* about being part of the church. And that is a big difference. It changes the situation radically because it forces churches to deal with something that they have wanted to avoid.

Even if there is no specific tradition about how to be gay or lesbian and Christian, however, there is a long tradition within Christianity about living a life of integrity, a life of hope, a life in loving communion with God and with our neighbors. The basic principles of this tradition, the guideposts of Christian spirituality, have as much to offer to lesbians and gay men as to anyone else. The difference is that, in the past, churches discouraged us from bringing our full lives into direct relationship with these principles. The whole erotic side of human existence, in our case, was forbidden. The result was to make any real spirituality very difficult to formulate. Now that we have begun to bring our whole selves into relationship with the gospel, we open up all sorts of new possibilities.

Vocation is about how we find the meaning in our own lives. It gives us the opportunity to discover God's grace anew in our own context. We can learn a good deal from the past, but what we learn has meaning only insofar as we can link it to our own experience. Neither our experience nor the tradition is enough by itself. Both can be distorted. Both can do evil as well as good. We can interpret our own experience in merely self-serving ways. Or we can make the tradition an instrument of repression and marginalization and use it against those we do not like or understand. Only when tradition and experience come into dialogue with each other and with God do we find out who we really are.

But vocation is not just about ourselves. It is also about how we contribute to the larger world. What we bring, in the long run, to both our communities—the gay-lesbian community and the church—will be the result of our own spiritual growth. We blaze trails. We identify landmarks. We construct, in effect, a kind of map to allow two previously isolated realms of human experience and understanding to come into conversation with each other—to our own benefit and theirs.

There is risk in this enterprise and a strong possibility of pain from time to time. There is also the possibility of being surprised by the rediscovery of grace and the delight of a life in communion with the Love that underlies all reality.

Beginning to Relearn

Bill and M. R.: At the heart of this book is an attempt to begin relearning who we are as gay Christians. (Others may read it and gain insight, of course, but the clear priority is to be at the service of the gay and lesbian communities.) This is proactive rather than reactive, using gay experiences as the norm of gay interpretations, rather than trying to justify our existence to the majority community.

We make several assumptions in writing this book:

1. We will waste no time justifying our presence in the church. As baptized Christians, we ourselves *are* the church, and we are obviously here, as we always have been: end of statement.
2. We will accept our sexuality as the God-given gift it is, affirming that we are not defective heteros, or indeed heteros of any kind. We are perfectly normal gay people faithfully trying to live out the identity God has granted us.
3. We will make our own appropriation of Scripture, Christian tradition, and history. The Christian community itself began by successfully

appropriating Scriptures, traditions, and history that were not its
own, and that pattern has been consistently followed by other
minority groups. We will make this process conscious.
4.   We will treat being gay or lesbian as a vocation, on a par with other
     Christian vocations, and the coming-out process as a spiritual
     journey.
5.   We will invite gay culture itself into the Christian context. We will
     freely use gay language and jokes, be camp if we feel moved to be,
     and flame as freely as God's love does.
6.   In place of the church's treatment of us as sick, sinful, or unaccept-
     able, we will hold up a vision of gay and lesbian people as God's
     people, God's tribe, as much called and chosen as the tribes of Israel
     or the early church.

The cumulative result of this heady mixture of assumptions should
be a changed self-perception, an energetic appropriation of a legitimate
place in the church, even an altered presence in the religious communities of which we are part.

Final Aims

We have several final aims in this work. First, we will attempt to present actual examples of the ways in which gay and lesbian Christians can
appropriate and retell the biblical story and their own spiritual journeys to create dynamic images that will articulate our self-perception
without simply reacting to the images already used by the majority
community.

Second, we will attempt throughout to model what a proactive and
self-affirming approach to gay/lesbian spirituality might look or sound
like, in the hopes that it will tempt others to push the boundaries a little further over time, without falling back into the kind of self-justifi-
cation too frequently characteristic of gay Christians.

Third, and perhaps most risky in presenting this project, we will actually use the humor, the language, and the characteristic spirit of gay
gatherings themselves: the setting that has pervaded all of the classes,
courses, workshops, and retreats we have ever participated in and yet,
sadly, too often gets left out of the classroom itself, and most assuredly
out of the writing.

This will probably offend a number of serious, devoted, and genuinely conscientious Christians. This is unfortunate, but it does not
alter our approach. Call it a gesture toward real self-disclosure in place
of mere acceptability that we do not apologize. It is, in the end, what
this book is about: affirmation, not acceptability.

M. R.: A QUEER SORT OF JOURNEY

Beginning with the Personal

There is nothing remotely impersonal when gay or lesbian Christians begin to talk about the reality of their sexual and spiritual unfolding, no matter how hard they try to tidy it up with objective language. That much said, I will admit that I can't be entirely objective when I speak about my own journey from inside the deepest perceptions of myself to the scary step of coming out some forty years ago, or about the strange circular journey that has taken me first out of Christianity in my teens and back into its embrace at forty and has drawn me from the deep and erotic mysticism of the Sufi/Hanafiyya tradition to the sexually troubled and conflicted Episcopal Church.

This is highly personal, of course, but then one's sexual identity is highly personal, and self-affirming gay or lesbian Christian identity really does have to begin with the self. Part of our simplest task in building a healthy sense of ourselves as a people—God's gay tribe, if you will—is to begin by sharing and weaving together the fabric of common stories, common histories, which reflect the fact that ours are not simply the sagas of flawed individuals, but a collective history of courage, persistence, and the irrepressible yearning for full selfhood.

Like that of most gay men and lesbians, my personal history doesn't come out sounding quite that grand. My story is too full of the gay people and gay places that shaped me, the campiness filled my humor and my life, and—lest I set aside the most essential and honest piece of all—the genuine queerness with which God has touched my life, and the genuinely queer sort of God this God has turned out to be.

This is apt to put off non-gay readers, but in telling our histories to ourselves, it is honesty that will speak most persuasively, and gay men and lesbians will recognize the truth of the story and the settings. There is, for example, the fact that one of my most reliable spiritual advisers and inspirations was a drag queen named Teddy, who held forth in a bar in Venice, California, and went to Mass every Sunday dressed (in Teddy's own words) "like a perfect lady," including pumps, hat, and gloves. Teddy found it amusing that the elderly parish priest, who obviously took Teddy for a woman, regarded her as a good example for the younger women who were too casual in their jeans and cut-offs. Teddy was, however, perfectly serious about attending Mass and receiving communion. "Honey, God knows who I am," Teddy said one day. "If I showed up trying to look like Mr. Macho Man, God would know I was trying to lie to him." There was real spiritual courage in Teddy's presenting herself before God in the simple, inescapable reality of her cross-dressing soul.

The simple fact is that most of our stories are full of odd and delicious details of that sort, and as long as we hesitate to fold them into our personal histories, we are still excluding a large part of ourselves and our culture. As long as we fear to name those parts of our stories, we will continue to attenuate our spiritual identity.

I will try, however, to move outside the mere outlines of my somewhat strange personal story, to invite other lesbians and gay Christians to contemplate the similarities their own stories may bear, no matter how much the surface differs. Most of us are, after all, shaped by the same culture, if not the same religion.

A Typical Story of a Very Certain Type

My story is one of those we are apt to call typically American, with one notable kink in the center of the pattern that has made my life very far indeed from what Americans born before World War II consider normal. My sexual identity and my spiritual identity have been intimately intertwined throughout my life, although one has been a great deal more changeable than the other. The changeable one, needless to say, was not my sexuality: that was crystal clear to me long before I even had words with which to label myself.

I am a first-generation Hungarian-American born in Cleveland, Ohio, in what was then the largest Hungarian community in the world outside Hungary. Like a large section of the pre-war American population, my world was urban, working class, and ethnic (and this, of course, is one of the typical features of my story). Mine was primarily a Roman Catholic neighborhood, although my own family held a mixed bag of religious backgrounds.

My mother's family was Hungarian Reformed. (The idea of reforming a Hungarian—particularly a gay one—has always struck me as vaguely ridiculous.) This very Protestant denomination, more Zwinglian than Calvinist, was rich in individual responsibility and piety, steeped in the conviction of *sola scriptura*, and morally austere. On the other side of the family, my grandmother was a devout Roman Catholic, all too typical of the elderly women we secretly referred to as "the black widows." Almost omnipresent in Eastern European neighborhoods, they dressed entirely in black, including black shawls and black woolen stockings, and carried rosaries with enormous black wooden beads. Part of my father's family was Serbian Orthodox, though family tradition has it that when my grandfather said he was going out to "make the stations," he meant hitting every bar on Buckeye Road, and he had no use whatever for churches of any kind. My parents were equally skeptical of religious authority and did not encourage my brother and me to follow it sheepishly.

Despite this somewhat troubled religious atmosphere, I was strongly attracted to things spiritual, even though often this involved walking a minefield of conflicting family sensibilities. At the age of nine, while sitting in the narrow strip of backyard behind the company housing my grandparents lived in, playing with a jackknife, I had a sudden and quite powerful conviction that I was going to grow up to be a preacher. Fortunately, I said nothing at the time, being too used to being told that no, I could not be a garbage truck driver, a Marine, a circus performer, or a lion hunter. Consequently, I managed to forget about it for some thirty years, without any regrets or sense of deprivation, until it overtook me when it was terrifyingly possible that a preacher was exactly what I would become.

An Oddity at the Center

I always knew, however, that there was something different about me, and certainly I had it pointed out to me on numerous occasions that I was weird (the word queer hadn't yet entered into my awareness), but no one was specific about exactly how I was weird. I do recall one of my earliest memories of being in school, probably in kindergarten, and of the teacher dividing the classroom up, asking all the little girls to stand on one side of the room and all the little boys on the other. A little boy named Stevie and I remained standing in the middle of the room as if marooned there, looking at both sides with some confusion, and knowing we didn't belong on either side. The teacher briskly shooed us to what she assumed was the proper side for each of us, but it was a surprisingly painful experience, a sense of having been blotted out of existence. No one saw me, or at least they didn't see who I was. I, on the other hand, saw who I was but had no word for it. I wavered between strongly suspecting that there was something wrong with the way I saw myself and the rock-bottom conviction that I really did know who I was, I really was different, and the flaw was in the vision of those who could not see me.

My active churchgoing stopped at age thirteen, and I stumbled into my teens with the sense that I was wildly out of place wherever I was. The obligatory junior-high and high-school dating mentality seemed quite bizarre to me, and like many gay teenagers, I retreated far into myself, experiencing a painful isolation that would leave me only in my thirties, and returns even now to haunt me.

On Labor Day weekend, 1959, at the ripe old age of eighteen, I came out, though it was already fairly old news to me. I had been falling in love with older women—as elderly as twenty-five, in fact—for years. I still had no word for it, but was oddly happy that way. It was certainly far more satisfactory than falling madly in love with an eighteen-year-old male. (My apologies here to my gay brothers who did precisely that.)

A World of My Own

The gay world I first knew was the world of ten years before Stonewall, of dismal little bars in Kent, Ohio, and Akron, Ohio, and the unspoken fear that the police might hit the bar at any time—bad enough if you were underage, but completely disastrous if you were to add gay into the bargain.

My spiritual life was a good match for the gay bars of Akron: it was uneasy, confused, and rootless, as I sought for something I could believe in, that would make sense of the person I was. Most of the religions I had brushed against had simply convinced me that they were designed for other people, but certainly not me. I had a fairly long period of flirtation with Eastern religions and something that was several decades too early to be called New Age, all of which were interesting, but none of which reached the center of myself.

It was not until I encountered a small pamphlet by a man named André Fikri that something gripped me hard enough to shake me to my roots. It was a simple parable:

FOLLOWING THE WAY

This is the lesson on following the way. Remember it.

> How do you follow the Way?
>> Go where you are sent.
>> Wait till you are shown what to do.
>> Do it with the whole self.
>> Remain till you have done what you were sent to do.
>> Walk away with empty hands.

How much will it cost?
The cost is everything, for all you are and all you have will be
asked of you before the journey runs it course.

How will you know your fellow travelers?
Their faces are marked by the scars of love.

No one will ever tell you that the Way is easy: only that it
is possible.

No one can tell you if the journey is worthwhile, for your wages are
concealed in the hand of God, and will be shown you only on
the last day of eternity.

But whoever chooses to follow the Way will have the joyous company of God's beloved fools as fellow travelers, and a resting
place, at journey's end, in the Mecca of the heart.

This is the lesson on following the Way. Remember it.[1]

I knew that whatever spiritual sanity I could find was there, embedded in the mystical tradition of Islam that André Fikri represented, a
framework at once dizzyingly freeing and reassuringly disciplined,
rooted in a long tradition but unafraid of pushing out beyond its
boundaries. The years I spent studying with him brought together all
the disparate pieces of myself, both spiritually and sexually—for André
Fikri was gay, and he was convinced that only someone who was gay or
lesbian could overcome the crippling effects of Western culture and religion and truly embrace the mystical path of the every day. The restruc-
turing of one's assumptions and personality would be too much for
anyone whose life was too satisfactory or intact. And of course, most
gay and lesbian people in our culture are not intact: there are enough
fractures in us that we are open to the movement of God.

He also believed that most Westerners' concept of their own sexuality
was so drastically attenuated that it was almost impossible to find someone who was able to step outside the boundaries of what was considered
masculine or feminine to embrace the boundless androgyny of God.

That was my life: what I lived, what I taught, what I wrote, and what
I was shaped by for years. Like anything that one has lived profoundly,
on some level it is indelible, and colors even what I understand of
Christianity and of myself as a Christian. It stayed with me, this conviction that God had a use for my brokenness and my oddly bigendered
nature. (The word "bigendered" is unfamiliar to many people, who con-
fuse it with either bisexual or transgendered. I am not even remotely

heterosexual, and I have exactly the gender that suits me. It just happens to be a bit less one-sided than most.)

As the seventies ended and the chill of the eighties began to settle on the subculture I knew, I found myself less and less comfortable in gay bars, gay ghettos, and gay politics. The trouble, I sensed, was not political but spiritual, and sent me off on a new journey, leading me first into the Religious Society of Friends (Quakers), the only place I felt absolutely safe. I had met Friends in the civil rights movement during the sixties, and I knew no one would ever pressure me against my conscience or insist that I hear God's voice in any way but my own. I was even asked to served on a committee studying the question of whether one had to be a Christian to be a Quaker. This was a very big question in the Society of Friends on the West Coast (still is), and I found myself having to look again at Christianity. It was like peeling off scabs, a combination of deep pain and anger, and even deeper yearning.

A Decidedly Queer Turn

On the day before my fortieth birthday, I was looking for an Al-Anon meeting, and I thought my little directory said St. Augustine's Episcopal Church, 12:00. It actually said 2:00, but I went over at noon to the basement of the church, found nobody there, and wandered around, finally locating an elevator. It took me up to a small corridor, which I followed. And suddenly there I was in the old choir section behind the altar, looking up at a forty-foot stained glass window of Christ.

I was horrified. All I could think of was escaping. But as I walked down the nave toward the door, I had an overwhelming experience of God, as powerful as if a voice had said, "Go where you are sent." This was somewhat dismaying for a gay woman who had spent the last couple of decades in the counterculture. I firmly believed that all Episcopalians were Republicans, that they starched their underwear, and that they never smiled. (A fair number of Episcopalians do, in fact, fit that description, but the church is a good deal more lively and diverse than that.) And yet I had an overwhelming sense that this is where God wanted me. Fortunately, I discovered that one of the parish priests was Malcolm Boyd, a man I had always admired for his courage in breaking the molds, working for civil rights and against war, and—perhaps most important—for coming out as a gay man. Our friendship was a treasure that continues to nourish me.

I recognize that this is a decidedly queer story, but it also seems right that it should be. I arrived in the church after more than twenty years of knowing I was gay and pursuing a spiritual life that articulated it.

Because I had spent so many years outside the mainstream, I wasn't aware that both my gender and my sexual identity were such problems for the church. But I had begun to outgrow the confines of the community I'd lived in and wanted the space to be found outside that world, however uncomfortable or risky it was.

So I came to the Episcopal Church, having come to terms with who I was outside the church's teaching (or mis-teaching) about sexuality. It was perhaps the most important gift I brought with me. It was simply too late for the church to tell me there was something spiritually wrong with me or my relationship to God. I came with too keen a sense of how rich my life had been, of all the gifts that gay men and lesbians had spiritually, and above all, how close, deep, and sustaining my relationship with God was. I didn't even know there was a problem with women as spiritual leaders until I got to the church. When you live on the fringe you are far less dependent on getting anyone else's permission to exercise your own gifts.

I was not convinced that I either had a problem or was a problem. I saw clearly that others had a problem with me, but their view seemed merely quaint and ignorant. To judge by the richness of my spiritual life, God did not have a problem with me. I believed then and believe now that I was born gay by the grace of God, and that God found this good, as God found all of creation good. If I still feel somewhat astonished at having ended up as an Episcopal priest, there is something decidedly right as well as decidedly queer about the thought. It is simply grace.

To say this all simply, since I don't believe that coincidence is anything but God's way of maintaining a low profile, there is great good sense in my bringing my twenty-plus years of spiritual adventure into the church. This is particularly true of the tradition (common to both the Quakers and the Fayyad'din Order) that gives the primary place to one's personal experience of God, rather than deferring to others' interpretations. The certainty that experience has given me has been a source of freedom for other gay and lesbian Christians, and it seems to be the greatest gift that many of us can bring back into the community of the church.

Finding a Place in the Church

Whatever the difficulties the church at large has with the issue of gay and lesbian Christians, there are vibrant and affirming oases within it, missions and parishes that embrace and welcome gay and lesbian Christians, and both listen and respond to the growing confidence of men and women who refuse to believe that God abhors what God has created.

In my case, I serve at a parish called St. Gregory Nyssen in San Francisco, a unique and creative setting in which no one will ever ask if you're gay or straight. Significantly, it is also a parish in which a large number of people have had spiritual journeys outside the mainstream of American religion, a place of "hyphenated Christians": Buddhist-, Jewish-, New Age-, and retro-Christians of every variety. There is, I believe, a strong connection between its willingness to serve as a place where people make bridges between the various parts of their spiritual journeys and its willingness to embrace those whose journeys have been entirely outside the mainstream. It is, perhaps, similar to what the church was originally: the table to which Jesus so freely invited everyone, rather than the tight little community in which all maintained a rigid similarity.

The open reentry of gay and lesbian people into the public life of the Christian community is a healthy return to the vitality of the early church, in which the boundaries of the legalistic first-century Hebrew religion had to be enlarged to include the despised Gentiles as equals. This, at least in part, is what the stories of gay and lesbian Christians in the twenty-first century will be about: the enlarging of the tent's borders, the enriching of the community's fabric. It is also about vocally claiming a separate and legitimate identity in the church: not simply flawed heterosexuals, but God's gay people, God's gay tribe, bearing gifts the church truly needs, even when it least wants them.

Another piece has to be kept in mind by those who take Christianity seriously: a kind of compassion and tenderness not only for the wounds that gay men and lesbians carry, but also for the people whose blindness and fear are so monstrous that they are led to demonize us. It is easier to survive being a target than it is to harbor the kind of hatred and fear that fuels homophobia.

All this is very personal. But that, in fact, is how gay spirituality and gay theology must proceed: we cannot be separated from the power of who we are and the stories that have shaped us. We can awaken one another and the church only when we speak clearly, personally, and forcefully in the gay voices God has given us and stop apologizing for histories that are as queer as the God who instigated them.

BILL: FINDING THE GOOD NEWS OF BEING GAY

Unexpected Identities

As the twentieth century has drawn to a close and a new one replaces it, Christian churches have found themselves absorbed (and sometimes even trapped) in conflicts over gender and sexuality. Some have argued that these are distractions, that there are weightier issues of poverty and debt, ignorance, slavery, and genocide. Without denying the gravity of those issues, I think that the tensions about gender and sexuality also go to the root of our Christian faith. The issues that have been raised are not simply issues about the status of women or of gay and lesbian people, but are issues about what we understand to be central to Christian faith and our relationship with God. The central question is "What is the good news that Jesus came to convey to us and what is it for?" In other words, "What is your gospel?" The word *gospel*, of course, means "good news," so whatever your gospel is, it's got to be news—it can't be just the same old stuff—and it's got to be good. It's got to make a positive difference in your life. If it's not making a positive difference in your life, it can't be gospel.

The good news is something that we can learn only in terms of our particular life experience, and mine is quite different from M. R.'s—and yet related. I'm an academic—a professor of biblical studies, specializing in New Testament, at The Church Divinity School of the Pacific, the Episcopal seminary in Berkeley, California. We are part of the Graduate Theological Union, a consortium of nine seminaries (Protestant, Anglican, Roman Catholic, and Unitarian, with centers for Jewish and Buddhist studies as well). I am also a priest in the Episcopal Church, and I help out at Good Shepherd Episcopal Church in Berkeley, a small congregation where, some time in the past ten years or so, we quit counting up who was gay and who was straight because sexual orientation no longer seemed like one of the primary distinguishing things about people in the congregation. It's not the only such place in the world, but it's rarer than I wish it were.

This is a very different world from the one I grew up in. I was born in
Oklahoma City in 1941 and grew up there. In some ways, Oklahoma is
one of the more conservative parts of the United States, though it's a
region apart. It's not exactly southern; it's not exactly western. It has a
distinctive history because it was long a kind of "dumping ground" for
Native American tribes that European-Americans wanted to evict from
places they coveted—until finally they decided that they coveted
Oklahoma, too. But Oklahoma is certainly one of the more conservative
states; and I did much of my growing up in the Eisenhower years, which
were a very conservative period in United States history. Those were also
the McCarthy years. Senator McCarthy of Wisconsin was on a rampage
against communists, looking for a communist sympathizer under every
bed. As far as he was concerned, gay men were essentially the same as
communists. It was a very repressive period for gay and lesbian people.
Growing up in Oklahoma, I didn't even know there were such people. I
had no concepts that would help me sort out my own sexual feelings as
they began to emerge. Eventually, I did what I was supposed to do as a
faithful son of Oklahoma in that time—I got married.

While I lived a heterosexual life for many years, it was based on a sense
of duty, not on sexual attraction. I have always been strongly oriented
to men in terms of erotic attraction, the depth and intensity of erotic
feeling. I have always enjoyed the company of women, but I am attracted
to men. And that was something I had no way, in that part of my life, of
figuring out—much less knowing what it was about. I put it down, I
suppose, as one of the many ways in which I was "odd" as a child. I was
bookish and bright. I didn't care for sports and wasn't good at them. I
was inquisitive and loved to learn. None of these things were thought
really appropriate for a boy in Oklahoma in the forties and fifties. I discovered classical music on the radio and had great enthusiasm for it. So
when I couldn't really *feel* why girls were supposed to be so fascinating,
I figured that, well, that was just part of the same thing. I didn't fulfill
any of the standard expectations well. But if I'd just get on with life, I
thought, I might not do the greatest job in the world, but I would manage. The idea that there might be other ways of explaining my difference
or, indeed, of viewing human life, simply didn't occur to me.

Ironically, the Stonewall Riots happened while I was on my honeymoon. I remember reading about them in the newspaper and thinking,
"They can't do that." But the questions of why they thought they *could*
do that and what, exactly, they thought they were doing stuck with me,
inescapably. Over the next fifteen years or so I came to the point where
I realized that I was, in fact, homosexual and that I was going to have
to deal with that.

When I was first able to say to myself, "I think I'm homosexual," I
thought, *Well, that's kind of an alarming discovery, but it's okay. Now that*

I know about it, it doesn't have to make any difference. After all, it's been true all my life, and I've managed to do what was expected of me anyway. I'll just continue to lead my life as I have. That worked for about eight months, and then I began to realize it was not going to work much longer. There were whole realms of emotional experience that I had buried, that I had not been dealing with; and, of course, emotions that are repressed tend to come back round and bite you on the butt. By the time they do, they have usually grown and transmogrified and turned into some kind of monster. I was lucky that it was no more difficult for me than it was, but I certainly had some confusing and frustrating years trying to figure out what this was going to mean for my life. It was a bit like having to go through adolescence in my thirties. Even when we've accumulated a good deal of life experience in some areas, there's still no way, in our world, to keep adolescence from being a trial—in all senses of the word.

I came out to my wife, and she was understandably upset. By that time, our marriage was deeply strained in other respects—a fact to which we had both contributed, usually without knowing what we were doing. My sexual orientation was certainly one part of that. My wife, I think, had long been perplexed, even if unconsciously, that I did not bring the emotional energy to the relationship that she did. In any case, the marriage was not a good context to work through a major life-challenge, though we did make efforts. In the long run, it was probably a good thing when diverging career paths landed us a couple of thousand miles apart, which in turn made it easier to move toward divorce. Although I was deeply grieved at being separated for much of the year from our daughter, my principal reaction was relief. My world had become simpler. I was no longer trying to live out a prescribed manner of life that, at the worst, was completely unrelated to the structures of my deepest emotions. In some ways, my married self had been a kind of public, substitute self with which I had little relationship. After moving to California at age forty-one, I could begin to sort out what it meant to be an openly gay man.

This story is not an unusual one for gay men of my age group. But alongside it is another story that's also relevant to the present book. One of the things that was odd about me as a child and adolescent was my interest in church, which was more of a "girl's thing" than a "boy's thing" for teenagers in Oklahoma. Boys were not expected to be too religious unless they were aiming to become ministers, so I thought I must be aiming at that. What I really wanted was to be an archeologist, but I gave that up and decided that I would be a minister. I think I made that decision out of a sense of duty, but God has used it in life-giving ways for me—and, I hope, for others, too. Then, at some point or other, while I was still too young to have any clear notion about college, much less

graduate school, I came to the conviction that I would eventually like to
teach in a seminary. From age twelve on, that became my long-run goal.
Happily, it's proven to be a real vocation for me—a life-path in which I
have come more and more deeply into relationship with God and with
other people. As an added blessing, it's also something I really like doing.

Surprised by Grace

What I didn't intend to do was to teach New Testament. That's been one
of the Spirit's little jokes—one of those unintended things that turn out
to be blessings only over a period of time. I'm not the only person I
know who has experienced this kind of divine humor. Some years ago
I was presiding at the Eucharist at Good Shepherd. Our custom there
is to receive communion in a circle around the altar, and, while we're
still standing there, the presider extemporizes the thanksgiving prayer
after communion—usually making use of themes from the sermon. I
was doing this and, taking up the preacher's words, began the prayer,
"We thank you, God, for surprising us with grace." After the service, a
parishioner came up to me and said, "I probably shouldn't tell you this.
But, you know, when you prayed, 'Thank you, God, for surprising us
with grace,' my immediate internal reaction was, 'And please don't ever
do it again!'" The surprise often seems like anything but grace at the
time. But it can lead us to a place of unguessed joy and freedom.

I actually ended up as a New Testament scholar almost by accident,
though I soon found it deeply engaging. I hadn't been interested in the
scholarly New Testament studies of the sixties and seventies because
they seemed too far removed from any reading of the New Testament
from the context of faith. But my doctoral program required me to have
some expertise in the area, and as fate or providence would have it,
that's what I wound up teaching. Only gradually was I able to bring
together my academic reading of the New Testament with my reading
of it in and for the life of faith. And only then did I begin to discover
why the Spirit had been pushing me in this direction.

Discovering that I am gay and having to deal with that turned out to
be the same kind of grace-filled surprise. It was not something I would
have chosen for myself. Dealing with it, as a man of my place and time
and as a person of faith, was anything but simple; and it's been an ongoing process, not a matter of days or weeks or months. Yet, it's been an
enormous grace. Over my early years, my religion had become a religion of stasis, a religion of "Here is how things are supposed to be. Now
follow this set of rules." That just wouldn't work any more. It had to be
replaced by a religion of grace, by a religion of risky reliance on God, a
God I could not control, could not grab hold of, couldn't even predict

very well. This is a God who has a penchant for surprising us, sometimes in ways that are not really at all welcome in the beginning. And
this God wants, in response, not a religion of stasis, but a faith that can
cope with newness, change, and growth. At the same time, this disruptive experience yields a religion, a faith of depth—of deeper roots, of
greater confidence.

I sometimes wonder: Had I known earlier in my life that I was gay,
would I still be involved with the church? The church has not been easy
for gay and lesbian people to be involved with. It's amazing how many
of us have stuck with the churches over the years, when we were being
told, in effect, to disappear. Not surprisingly, a tremendous number of
gay and lesbian people want nothing to do with the church. But by the
time I was coming out, my identity as a Christian was already deeply
formed, and I had experienced its life-giving potential. There was no
way that I could simply walk away from it.

I knew from the beginning that I would have to work, to search, to discover how these two gifts from God related to each other. In some strange
way, I was never in any doubt that my sexuality and my awareness of that
sexuality were gifts from God. As soon as I acknowledged this sexuality,
life became clearer and simpler and richer, even though there was much
sorting out left to do. I had all kinds of energy—spiritually, intellectually,
and emotionally—that I hadn't experienced before because it was tied up
in concealing myself from myself. My sense of communion with God
deepened. And all of this was rooted in the experience of consenting to
a truth I had been avoiding. This could only be a gift of grace, and I
knew that I would be spending a big part of my life figuring out how
those two graces—the grace of Christian faith and the grace of being
gay—related to each other and how they could illuminate each other.

M. R.: A PEOPLE DEFINED BY DESIRE

Restating the Dilemma

Two of the questions that usually come up in the course of most workshops for gay and lesbian Christians are, "How do we as Christians bear witness to the wider gay community?" and "How do we as gay men and lesbians bear witness to the Christian community?" In other words, it's the double-headed dilemma most gay and lesbian Christians are aware of: our gay brothers and sisters don't trust us because we're Christians, while our Christian brothers and sisters don't trust us because we're gay. As it's usually stated, it appears insoluble, and so for that reason I am going to restate the issue in what are more appropriate terms.

Figuring out how to get gay and lesbian people to trust us, or Christian people to trust us, is entirely beside the point. It would of course be nice, or comfortable, or safer, or any number of things. But ultimately it is irrelevant. We need to look first at the ways in which we can trust our own perceptions of ourselves and our relationship to God and decide once and for all that apologizing for being who we are (both gay and Christian) is not only pointless, but unnecessary. God did not consult the hetero majority before creating us; it is in fact neither their place nor their privilege to demand that we justify our existence. The number of people who hold a particular point of view and the length of time over which they have held it is absolutely no indicator of either its truth or even its reasonableness. No amount of argument or pleading will alter the reality of things: the believers in a round earth did not destroy the flat earth. It had simply never existed in the first place.

Taking the High Ground

This is a point at which a certain amount of nerve, of courage, of holy *chutzpah* becomes necessary, not to mention a certain amount of honesty that may be quite unpalatable to many people. Personal statement: as a person who didn't set foot in the church until she was forty, and who arrived on the scene with a deep and lively trust in God, I don't really care whether the church accepts me or not: I'm here. And this is by no means merely a personal issue, but one of the communal realities we need to address. The time has come for gay and lesbian people as a community to give up the futile attempt to justify our existence in the church or in the world. We are here. We have always been here. The fact that most of the churches have lived in blissful ignorance of our presence means nothing. Our task—our ministry to ourselves and to the church—is not to justify our presence, but to tell the church who we really are by our own definitions, rather than by theirs, because we know who we are. And it is a kindness neither to them nor to us to continue pretending that they have any superior knowledge or authority on the subject.

In other words, it is time we took the high ground, and began reeducating ourselves to what the task really is. It is not for the church to admit us. The church did not call us; God did. It is not the church's gospel; it is Christ's. In asserting our right to the selfhood that God bestowed on us, we are not in fact threatening or attacking the church, the gospel, God, or Christ, but asserting the primacy of the creating God and the liberating news of Jesus Christ.

Granted, this is bound to upset the church a great deal, but the fact is that if the church is not upset, it is not doing its job. If there is not heated discussion going on in Christian communities about *something*, we are not following the gospel (that is, we are not allowing ourselves to be pushed beyond our comfort zone or our personal interest).

This is not the first issue that Christians thought the church would self-destruct over; it will certainly not be the last. We are actually a rather minor ripple in the stream. Wherever the gospel is truly preached and truly heard, contention follows. The gospels portray Jesus himself as unsparingly realistic about this:

> "I came to bring fire to the earth, and how I wish it were already kindled! I have a baptism with which to be baptized, and what stress I am under until it is completed! Do you think that I have come to bring peace to the earth? No, I tell you, but rather division! From now on five in one household will be divided, three against two and two against three; they will be divided: father against son and son against father, mother against daughter and daughter against mother, mother-in-law against her daughter-in-law and daughter-in-law against mother-in-law." *(Luke 12:49-53)*

> "Do not think that I have come to bring peace to the earth; I have not come to bring peace, but a sword. For I have come to set a man against his father, and a daughter against her mother,

and a daughter-in-law against her mother-in-law; and one's foes will be members of one's own household. Whoever loves father or mother more than me is not worthy of me; and whoever loves son or daughter more than me is not worthy of me; and whoever does not take up the cross and follow me is not worthy of me. Those who find their life will lose it, and those who lose their life for my sake will find it." *(Matthew 10:34-39)*

The gospel is not about smoothing over the issues that divide us, nor integration in the sense of making us all agree, think alike, or even worship alike. It is about affirming the godly identity of every human being, even those whom we find strange (or queer). Its work will continue until we can all take our places at the table without challenging anyone's right to be there. Whom God has called, no human being has the right to turn away.

As a gay woman, I have an equal responsibility for affirming straight people, though I do not pretend to understand what the world really looks like through their eyes. Their attitudes are foreign to me. Despite their dismal showing, I cannot demand that we declare a moratorium on ordaining married heterosexual men simply because they commit the vast majority of incidents of sexual misconduct in the church. Despite their corporate acts of injustice, oppression, and hatred, I am forced to take the gospel seriously and admit that heterosexuals are as apt to show saintliness as gay men and women. They do not need my permission to be baptized, communicated, blessed, or ordained.

What I propose, then, is not so much a process of integrating ourselves into the church, but a reintegration of our own way of conceptualizing the task. And it extends well beyond the gay and lesbian community. It is learning that would merit application to the church's racism, sexism, ageism, and assorted other -isms.

This is exactly the same thing that happens as the gospel works its way under the surface: we are confronted with our own limits, our own boundaries, until we find ourselves not just accommodating to those outside the walls, but breaking down the walls to embrace them. The gospel does not permit us to take it seriously and simultaneously remain blind to our complete mutuality with all other human beings. To quote my teacher, André Fikri, "No one walks out alone, ever." Our growth as Christians is tied to the community to which we belong and the growth of our brothers and sisters. We are not invited into a church where everyone is welcome but no real conversation takes place. We are invited to a community where we are all pressed to lifelong growth, which will necessarily involve stress, doubt, conflict, and relearning.

Being members of one minority does not excuse us from the task of accommodating others or absolve us from the sin of damaging other

minorities. Part of our task in the church is to begin to let the church
know who we really are, risky as it is. We must acknowledge that we are
at least partly responsible for the fact that so many Christians continue
to entertain the most appalling stereotypes about us. That can only end
as we become willing to show them our faces. They, in turn, have been
denied the knowledge that many people they have loved and admired
in the church are as gay as they come.

Life in the Discomfort Zone

One of the things that makes many people uncomfortable with having
gay and lesbian people in church in the first place is that we force them
to ask questions about themselves and their own sexuality. When you
come down to it, when does the church really talk about sex at all? If
we weren't there to make an occasion, straight Christians might go for
decades without having to mention it or think about it. And there are
far too many people who have been damaged by religious misteaching
about sexuality to allow that to stand unchallenged.

Among other things, we are there to put a face on the words "gay and
lesbian," but we are also a continual reminder that we are all born sexual: there is no getting away from it. Whether we're gay or straight, we
as a culture are obsessed with sex and almost terminally confused about
it. No one really grows up whole in our culture, especially when it
comes to sexuality. Even if you fit the approved pattern, have the ideal
marriage and the perfect Norman Rockwell family, you have probably
not escaped the problem. We have so separated sexuality and spirituality, so separated the spirit from the body, have become so divided
against ourselves, that there are huge parts of every one of us that we
have disowned. And as we disown parts of ourselves, we need people
on whom to project those disowned parts safely. As gay men and lesbians, we're it for the heterosexual culture. We are the safe space that
allows others to live with their own sexual tension, by projecting it onto
us and punishing it in us.

Earlier, I mentioned the card someone sent me blaring about "The Gay
Lifestyle." It merely pointed up the fact that the reality of most gay men's
and lesbians' sexuality is no more a part of their lives than it is for heterosexuals. We too live in a world that consists in large part of going to
work, cleaning the apartment, attending church, telephoning our relatives, and de-fleaing the dog. But the myth persists, even when you are
fifty-nine years old (as I am) and gave up going to bars years ago.

Still, there is something extremely important here, in a positive sense.
Think about this: we are not a minority defined by our race, national
origin, religion, or economic bracket. *We are a people defined by our*

desires. To put it in a more Christian way, we are defined by our loves. I recollect a hymn whose refrain is "They'll know we are Christians by our love." Well, we too know who we are by our loves. And there is something profoundly right about that. To be a woman defined by her desires, to be a man defined by his love, and to be faithful to those desires and that love, even in the face of everything that society and the church have done to us, is nothing short of awesome. It is something we have to offer others, a self-acknowledgment and self-affirmation that the rest of the church needs as desperately as we do.

The Passionate Word

Desire is so seldom permitted to ripple the surface of the church that it is a small wonder that many people dismiss religion as lifeless and boring. What an insult to the God who invented sexuality, to desire so little!

There is nothing unpassionate about the gospel, and nothing at all lukewarm about God's deep desire for mercy, justice, and love among human beings. If we have the chance to do anything, it is to remind the church that creation itself is rooted in God's desire, and that human beings, who are the image and likeness of God, are sexual beings who reflect God's passion and love.

This reminder is something else the gay and lesbian community can offer to the church. There are many Christian sisters and brothers who will find this offensive, but Jesus never claimed that he was not a cause for scandal among the righteous. The early church understood this, as well, recognizing that simply being a Christian would give offense to lots of people. We are standing in the very center of the tradition at the moment, whether we know it or not: the tradition of challenging the presuppositions about who belongs to God and who does not.

This is an ongoing tradition that has never purported to create the perfect or final community. Our vision will fall short, too. But in this time and in this place, we are the unpalatable cornerstone. Our offensive certainty of God's call to us is the strongest way in which we can truly keep faith with the early church. Without its willingness to offend the received wisdom of its world by preaching the outrageous gospel, we would not have a church at all.

Sexuality: Problem or Pure Gift?

How do we as gay men and lesbians begin to reeducate the church about the reality of our lives and the unreality of its perceptions about us? There is no simple answer, of course, but there are a few prescriptions I can

offer. First, we must stop worrying about whether the church can accept
or justify our presence and our desire to serve as priests, form lifelong
unions, and redefine the meaning of family. We must understand quite
clearly what is our problem and what is not, and politely but resolutely
hand the heterosexual community its problem back. Our love, our desire,
is not a problem, but a gift, one of the greatest pieces of God's grace we
can know.

Being gay is not a sin, nor a sickness, but God's gift to us. I frequently
annoy other church members because I insist on using the phrase that
"I was born gay by the grace of God." In other words, I do not believe
my sexuality was either an accident or a mistake. It deserves to be
rejoiced in. Many of us know, deep down, that being gay has pushed us
further, spiritually, than we might have gone if our lives had been more
comfortable. It has also made us understand love in profound ways that
we might not have felt otherwise. Perhaps even more important, it has
meant that we have had to come to a Christian identity that does not
pretend we are not sexual.

Will the church reverse its unconscionable injustice toward gay men
and lesbians? Will we soon have a truly loving Christian community in
which it won't matter if you're gay or straight? Probably not in our lifetimes. There will be places, as there always have been—parishes, dioceses, communities—in which we can be who we are. But there are lives
that can never be made whole, and losses that can never be regained.

There is not a single named gay man or lesbian person in the
Scriptures, either in the Old or New Testament. This is a genuine act
of psychic genocide, if you will, a process of having been blotted out
of existence so total in its intent that this part of our history can probably never be retrieved. Can anyone name any of Jesus' gay and lesbian disciples? No one will convince me that we were not there,
named or unnamed. We were there; we have always been there, recognized or not. We have paid our pledges, taught in Sunday schools,
laid down our lives in defense of others, fed the hungry, and—yes, in
the midst of it—made love to those of our own genders and built caring communities.

We deserve something better than mere assimilation: we deserve the
right to preserve our distinct identity in the midst of the church. No
one, gay or straight, was ever called to be a generic Christian. We have
been called to bring the totality of ourselves into the community, which
is precisely what has formed the richness of Christianity. The church
has gathered strange and contradictory elements and held them
together in a single community. It must never settle for being a club of
like-minded people, but a living organism in which opposites fight and
woo each other, and ultimately yield new beings.

A Modest Proposal

So here, it seems, is the task of gay and lesbian Christians who are serious about living out the gospel: don't burden your gay brothers and sisters by succumbing to the desire to justify your presence. It is the church's place to listen now, and ours to speak. And this is not merely about speaking the word of the gay community, it is about speaking the radical word of the gospel, which is about God's outrageous desire to include every variety of person we can think of, and then create yet more. The living church, like creation itself, is not as tidy as we think it ought to be. It is messily alive, and continually leaks out at the edges. That is probably the way God wanted it to be. Being alive is not about being a well-functioning machine, any more than being a church is about simply being an organization.

Being the church is about a force as strong as that which shook the disciples on the day of Pentecost, a roaring wind and a thunder of flaming spirit, a power that shakes us to the core and sends us out to change the world.

It is about desire.

It is about love.

BILL: THE CHURCH AND SEX—
A CHECKERED HISTORY

Change Is a Permanent Part of the Church

God has a strange propensity for creating new families out of groups of people who have nothing to do with each other. We usually think about the Exodus in terms of the offspring of Jacob—a single clan with a common ancestry—rising up and leaving Egypt, but there's one little verse in Exodus (12:38) that tells us that a mixed multitude went up with them. The ancestry of Israel isn't just the line of Jacob. It's the line of Jacob plus the offspring of the mixed multitude that left Egypt with them. An even more vivid example of this strange tendency is the creation of the church in the New Testament. The church began as a small Jewish sect, composed of people who shared a lot of common perceptions and presuppositions, and then God had the temerity to surprise that group of people by calling in *Gentiles*—people who were categorically "other than" Israel.

Some people were ready to accept that: "If this is who God calls, then we go along with it." Other people were not sure what they thought about it. And still others thought that God, as so often, was being very sloppy and that their job was to clean things up and get rid of the interlopers. A lot of the history that's recorded in the New Testament, both in the Acts of the Apostles and in Paul's letters, is the story of Paul and others resisting that attitude and saying, "No, if God wants Gentiles in the church, then God wants Gentiles in the church. God isn't just saying to the Gentiles, 'You can become Jews now, too.' God is saying, 'No, the church is going to be radically different from what you thought it was.'"

Henry Vaughan, a mid-seventeenth-century poet, makes this point in a stunning way. Here are the first few lines of his poem "Faith":

> Bright and blest beam! whose strong projection
>   Equal to all,
> Reacheth as well things of dejection
>   As the high and tall,

How hath my God by raying thee
Enlarged his spouse,
And of a private family
Made open house!

That's what the gospel does: it makes us pregnant with the unexpected
and opens up the tight boundaries of our existing communities. If the
church wants to go on being the church—being the community of the
gospel and not a cozy little sect (composed chiefly of heterosexual
Gentiles, now, rather than Jews)—then it's going to have to pay attention to that. We lesbian and gay folk are, in a sense, God's gift to the
church at the present moment, to help make that possible. If part of the
church does some kicking and screaming about it, that's nothing new.
It's just like what we read in the New Testament.

One of the important things to realize, when we get discouraged about
the glacial pace of change, is that it's just that—glacial. Ecclesiastical time
is a version of geological time. It's easy in a single human lifetime to get
the impression that nothing ever changes. Periodically, I have to stop
myself and think, "Okay, what was it like fifteen years ago?" Then I realize that a lot has changed in a fairly short period of time. We're way short
of where I would like us to be, but a lot has changed. Still, change in the
church tends to be slow. Maybe it's even more confusing than slow. It's
a little like recent conceptions of evolutionary time. It's not simply a
gradual, steady accumulation of events so much as it is a moment of crisis followed by a period of stasis, which is again followed by a moment of
crisis, when things may change rapidly, followed by another period of
stasis when things stay pretty much the same.

A result of this is that most of us assume that the church hardly ever
changes at all. But, in reality, the church has changed a great deal over the
ages. We are apt to have a mental image of the church from our early
childhood; in effect, it's the church of our grandparents' generation. And
then we assume that it was always that way—way back to the first century.
There may have been a few obvious differences. For example, martyrdom
existed in the first century, and in our grandparents' time martyrdom was
something practiced only by rather pale female relatives who were coz-
ened into it, or even forced into it by community consent, because somebody had to take care of great-grandmother and it wasn't going to be me.
That was the only kind of martyr the church of my childhood had.

But basically the assumption was that the church had always been the
same: Christian attitudes had always been the same. Christian doctrines
had always been the same. The faith had always been understood in the
same way. And, above all, the prevailing mores that determined whether
you're a respectable person or not—those had always been the same.

Well, it's not true.

This is a very difficult point to get across because few of us know much history, nor do we take it very seriously. In the United States, many of us have grown up in places that don't, in fact, have much history. I was born in 1941 in a city that had been founded in 1889; and it was one of the older cities in Oklahoma. Many people today grow up in suburbs that didn't exist fifty years ago.

Reclaiming History

One result of our historical short-sightedness is that many people in the U.S. assume that the fundamentalist version of Christianity is the same as the Christianity of Jesus and the disciples. This can come out occasionally in quite funny ways. A small-town school board back in the fifties banned the teaching of foreign languages because if English was good enough for Jesus and his disciples, it was good enough for the kids in that county. And quite recently, someone handed me an advertisement culled from a Fundamentalist magazine. It was addressed to people who were tired of having the "preserved word of God in the King James version" tampered with by clergy who quoted "the Greek and other translations."

I love that phrase, "preserved Word of God"; it sounds like it's been pickled in brine. But the really revealing remark is the strange reference to the Greek, the original language of the New Testament, as if it were somehow inferior to an English translation made from it. This extreme of ignorance becomes humorous, of course. But I think most people in the United States share the underlying, unreflective assumption that mean-spirited, legalistic Fundamentalism is the original version of Christianity, while the older, more historic traditions of Christian faith— Lutherans, Episcopalians, Roman Catholics, and so on—are compromise versions for people who are weak-kneed and can't quite take the original, rigorous version. Only Fundamentalists are really faithful to that.

Of course, there is no truth to this peculiar idea. The Fundamentalism we know today is of relatively recent origin. It's only about a hundred years old, and it arose out of tensions and pressures within the older denominations in the late nineteenth and early twentieth centuries. Like other religious fundamentalisms—Jewish, Muslim, Hindu—it represents a defensive reaction to the outside world on the part of faith communities that feel themselves, rightly or wrongly, to be threatened. There's a good, accessible history of Fundamentalism in Bruce Bawer's book *Stealing Jesus*. It's well worth reading to get a more accurate sense of what has created the current religious scene.

However much Christians may have wanted, over the centuries, to fix their life and faith in eternal forms, in actual practice, Christianity

changes enormously from one era to another. If you spend some concentrated time in another era of Christian history by reading the writings and looking at the material remains, you discover very quickly that
the preconceptions you brought with you don't work. The texts you're
reading don't quite make sense; the buildings and the art seem incomprehensible. Only gradually, as you read and study, do you discover that
early believers' understanding of Christian faith and life was not identical to yours. Sometimes the differences are quite striking. Sometimes
they're so subtle that they're very hard to trace. But they're always there.

Sex Rears Its Lovely Head

One thing about Christianity that's particularly significant for us in the
present context is that the church has long been deeply suspicious of
sex. This is one of the reasons why gay and lesbian people pose such a
particular challenge to Christians today. It's a challenge not unlike that
of women's liberation. One of the reasons the ordination of women to
the priesthood in the Episcopal Church created such anxiety for a lot
of people had to do with sex. I heard more than one person say, "But
what if she's pregnant?" With a pregnant woman standing at the altar,
it's hard to avoid noticing that she must have had sex at some point.
You could perhaps ignore the fact that the male priest's wife is pregnant, because she's probably sitting in the back row anyway, but you
can't ignore the pregnant woman who's presiding at the altar.

This anxiety about sex has taken different forms over the ages. It's an
old anxiety; but, oddly enough, it's not particularly strong in the New
Testament. You can read it back into the New Testament by emphasizing the passages that seem to have a special interest in it. But it was really
the second and third centuries that made it a central concern—and for
reasons that we probably wouldn't suspect now. There is an odd passage
in three of the Gospels (Mark 12:25; Matthew 22:30; Luke 20:35) in
which Jesus is talking with some Sadducees about the issue of life after
death. They have proposed to him a complicated question about marriage and family responsibilities in the age to come. He replies, "Don't
you know that in the life after death they neither marry nor are given in
marriage?" People often read the passage as saying there is no sex in
heaven, but what it really says is that there is no marriage in heaven,
which is a little different. And the reason given is this: "They neither
marry nor are given in marriage, but they are like the angels of God."

In later Christian thought, angels are sexless beings, which reinforces
the idea that there's no sex in heaven, but they were not viewed that way
in first-century Christian thought. Think, for example, of the little letter of Jude, where it appears that early Christians were teaching that you

needed to have sex with angels in order to gain high standing in heaven. Jude refers to this teaching only in veiled ways, but that is what he's attacking. Of course, his readers knew the Hebrew Bible (mostly in Greek translation), and they knew the story in Genesis 6:1–4 about angels having sex with human women and the offspring being giants. Jude refers to that story and also to the story of the men of Sodom who "in the same manner" as these angels" went after strange flesh" (Jude 7 AV, referring to Genesis 18). Far from thinking that the sin of Sodom had to do with male homosexuality, Jude thought it was about human beings wanting to have sex with angels. So the earliest Christians didn't assume that angels were sexless.

Jesus' point in the Gospels is not that angels are sexless, but that they live forever. Luke's version makes that clear: "Indeed they cannot die anymore, because they are like angels in heaven" (Luke 20:36). If you live forever, you don't need children; and if you don't need children, you don't need marriage. At least, this was how it looked in the first-century world. The family was the basic social unit. Children were a way of perpetuating the family. Marriage ensured the existence and the legitimacy of heirs. All of these are familiar words for us today: children, family, marriage, angels, and so on. But if you put them back into a first-century context, you find they can also be quite unfamiliar. When Christians of the second century began to say that Christians have to give up sex, the basis of their argument was not that sex is inherently bad, but that you're going to live forever and therefore don't need offspring. Marriage, family, and children are entanglements with *this* world. *You're* going to be like the angels in heaven. The early Christian movement known as Encratism (which means something like "Self-control-ism") was founded on this kind of reasoning. Who'd have thought it?

Early Sexual "Freedom"

The second-century rejection of marriage and procreation probably seemed like a moment of liberation for many early Christians. They were freeing themselves from the meaningless demands of the present world. Another reason celibacy became terribly important in early Christianity is that vows of virginity gave women in the first and second century a freedom that they could not have in any other way. In the ancient Mediterranean world, women were the property of their fathers. The father was the embodiment of the family; he was not functioning like a modern individual in this role. And his daughters belonged to him, as head of the family. He could give them away in marriage in exchange for desirable family connections, specific commitments, or other goods. At that point, the woman became the property of her husband as a sort of quasi-member of his family. She didn't truly become a part of that family until her husband died and her son succeeded as head of the household. She was then part of her son's family. But if she were divorced before that, she was sent back to her family of origin, while her children stayed with their father. They were *his* offspring, who existed for the benefit of his family.

The one stage in which a woman might have some freedom of her own was widowhood—and then only if she had the resources to maintain a relatively secure and comfortable existence. From the early second century onward, Christianity was able to offer women another opportunity to have some control: they could vow virginity and, under God's protection, take themselves out of the whole family orbit. They often continued to live in their parents' house, but they were no longer under the father's authority in the same way. In this way, Christians were able to honor the spiritual equality of men and women in a world that made that difficult.

Solutions Can Become Problems

But one era's solution can become the next era's problem. Has virginity always been a way of emancipating women? It may have worked for a long time. It's sometimes said that the Reformation actually meant a loss of spiritual status for women in Protestant countries, because there was no longer any institution in which women could lead and enjoy authority after the abolition of the religious orders. From then on they could only be wives or spinsters; those were the only functions allotted to them. In our own century, however, the Roman Catholic nuns who left their religious communities after Vatican II probably didn't see their religious orders as opportunities for liberation. In some cases, those orders had rigidified into repressive institutions that subordinated most of the members to an existence that no longer seemed clearly meaningful. One positive consequence of that era has been a strong movement among women religious to rediscover and reclaim the positive elements that originally made such a life attractive to Christian women.

The solution of one era can become the problem of another. To bring it a little closer to home for many of us: where did the sometimes tyrannical notion of family in the middle part of the last century come from? The image of family that confined women to the home, that created a high level of anxiety about all forms of human life other than the nuclear family? This had a lot of sanction from churches: "The family that prays together, stays together." All church activity was oriented toward families, as it still is in many cases. Single people often have difficulty feeling that there's any place for them in Christian congregations. This notion of family, which makes everyone who is not a member of a family in this particular sense a question mark, is not ancient in Western culture, and it's certainly not biblical.

It's comical, really, when people describe the mid-twentieth-century household in terms of "biblical family values." The biblical family was typically a polygamous household. The stories of incest and mayhem are numerous. And in fact the household was much larger than just the people who were biologically related to one another. It typically included slaves and assorted hangers-on. The slaves were as much a part of the family as anybody else, even though in a way very disadvantageous to them. When I first studied Latin, as a teenager, I was perplexed by the word for children, *liberi*—always in the plural and meaning, literally, "free ones." Paul explains the social background of that terminology when he says that as long as the child is a minor, his or her status is the same as that of a slave (Galatians 4:1). So how do you distinguish all these underlings at the bottom of the household heap? Well, there are the *liberi*, the free ones, who will grow up to inherit, and there are the *servi*, who will stay slaves all their lives. They never explained that to me in high-school Latin!

Our modern focus on the nuclear family arose only in the Victorian era, and it came out of Victorian reform movements, whose goal was to improve the status of women. Women in the early nineteenth century had virtually no legal rights and were often treated as not much better than serfs. The Victorian reformers tried to change that by emphasizing the woman's role as spiritual center of the nuclear family. Women were to be put on a pedestal as a defense against their being treated like dirt. Unfortunately, a pedestal is also confining. Women's liberation has attacked this identification between "woman" and "mother" as a kind of slavery. But in the nineteenth-century context, it looked like the solution of some significant problems.

A Long and Checkered History

Although we are apt to imagine the church as something absolutely unchanging over the ages, particularly on the subject of sex, in reality, it has been in constant motion throughout its history. The motion is sufficiently glacial in its pace that we're often unaware of it, but the church is not monolithic, and the Christian religion has not in fact remained exactly the same from one period to the next. Even if the tradition has been suspicious of sexuality on the whole, the precise character of that suspicion has changed a good deal. The first enthusiasm for virginity in the second and third centuries was primarily an attack on the family as too entangled with the world. By the fifth century, Christians had pretty much agreed that celibacy was superior to family life, but that didn't mean that most Christians were going to be celibate. Family life was the usual pattern, though it was often seen as lacking in religious seriousness.

In the twelfth century, Western monks led a movement hoping to give family life religious value by arguing that it could be a school of virtue, not unlike the monastery. About the same time, the church was beginning to interest itself in the question of marriage, which it had never gotten much involved with before. Only in the eleventh and twelfth centuries did marriage begin to be considered a sacrament of the church. And only then did the church begin to have a real role in it. The main reason appears to be that, as life became more settled, the aristocracy of western Europe decided that the question of who owned what piece of property could perhaps be settled without always having to bash your neighbor in the head. One way to do it was through the marriage game. But if the marriage game was going to have such high stakes, there had to be impartial referees—a role assumed by the church. Yet, even then, you couldn't get married *in* a church. You could get married in the church porch; they weren't sanctifying any of that sex stuff inside the consecrated building, thank you very much.

So there's been a history of negotiation and renegotiation, of constant shifting back and forth about sex within the history of Christianity. One such shift took place as late as the eighteenth century, when sex began to become the kind of dirty secret it remained up until the sixties of the twentieth century. In the middle of the eighteenth century, the English composer William Boyce wrote an oratorio called "Solomon." The text, by an Irish poet named Edward Moore, was simply a paraphrase of the Song of Solomon in the Bible. It's a very sexy paraphrase, but given the age-old tendency to take the Song of Solomon allegorically as a song of the love of God for Israel, or the love of Christ for the Church, or the love of God for the individual soul, it was still possible, in the middle of the eighteenth century, to create a work that could be read or heard as both erotic and spiritual. By the end of the eighteenth century, however, "Solomon" had become a hot potato. The music was and is gorgeous, but people quit performing it because audiences couldn't handle that text anymore.

Outcasts from the Garden of Love

A poem by William Blake describes this shift and attacks the church for it. It's called "The Garden of Love":

I went to the Garden of Love,
And saw what I never had seen:
A Chapel was built in the midst,
Where I used to play on the green.

And the gates of this Chapel were shut,
and "Thou shalt not" writ over the door;
So I turned to the Garden of Love
That so many sweet flowers bore;

And I saw it was filled with graves,
And tombstones where flowers should be;
And Priests in black gowns were walking their rounds
And binding with briars my joys and desires.

That's what the church looked like to Blake at the end of the eighteenth century. It looked like that to a lot of other people, too.

It's worth observing that there are really two distressing things going on in the poem. First, there is a chapel in the middle of the green. The poet is surprised to see it, but he's not particularly hostile about it. The evil thing is that the chapel is shut; it's locked; nobody can go into it. And its meaning is defined in purely negative terms: "Thou shalt not." But then, when he turns to the garden of love that "so many sweet flowers bore," he finds that even it is now "filled with graves." The priests don't want you to get too close to your desires, and they don't want you to get too close to God, either. Even the *sound* of those last two lines, which are longer than the preceding ones, seems to erect a wall of exclusion.

Blake's poem is reminiscent of the passage in the Gospel of Luke (11:46), in which Jesus rebukes the religious authorities of his day because "you load people with burdens hard to bear, and you yourself do not lift a finger to ease them." Religion, useful though it is in many ways, is always tempted to impose itself between the worshiper and God. Religion— Christian religion along with the rest—has embedded in it this tendency to want not just to point you toward God, but to *be* your God. A colleague of mine had a Jewish grandmother who said to him when he was quite young, "Be careful about religion when it tries to take the place of God." Christian style is often too polite to say that so bluntly, but Judaism has cultivated an admirable ability to speak the truth even about religion. Be careful about religion—it keeps trying to take the place of God. One of the ways it does that is to interpose itself between you and God—to make your view or your vision stop at the chapel instead of passing through the chapel. In fact, it may not even want to let you into the chapel until you've proved how very, very good you are.

Putting the Church in its Place

There is a story about one of the founders of what is now the Christian Church (Disciples of Christ), Alexander Campbell, and how he rejected this kind of thinking. He belonged to a very strict, dissenting Presbyterian Church in Ireland. When members there were going to receive communion they had to be interviewed by the Board of Elders to make sure that their doctrine was sound and that they weren't violating the discipline of the church, and then they would be given a token, which they could lay on the communion table and then they could receive communion. Campbell went through the whole process, received his token, walked up to the communion table, laid the token on the table, and then walked out without receiving. He had realized that this was Jesus' table, not the church's table—and that many of Jesus' original followers might well have been rejected by the elders of his own time. That was a moment of discovery for him, that the church is not God. The church can't keep you away from God, though it surely can try. It will even try to persuade you that it really does have the power to keep you away from God. But it really can't do that, even though it can construct all these barriers and bind with briars your joys and desires.

The church didn't call us. God called us. The Spirit, playing her little joke on us *and* on the church, has sometimes called us to churches that don't want us. But that's how God operates—with a sense of humor that is pervasive and sometimes a little difficult to follow and often terribly inconvenient for the time being. We need to accept the fact that we've been called and that we have a place here whether or not the person next to us in the pew feels altogether comfortable about it. And then we also need to take another step and recognize that the church is not set in concrete. It is, at most, carved in mashed potatoes. Now, the church's mashed potatoes frequently seem like concrete because they've been sitting there a long time (though not as long as many would like you to believe). The church may *seem* quite petrified, but it's not. And even if it were, that would only be all the more reason to say "We need to have some change here. The Spirit wants us to have room to breathe." If the church starts worshiping itself, if the church thinks it has reached perfection, that's an absolutely certain sign that it has betrayed its true vocation.

I suspect that part of the big joke that God is playing on the world we live in right now is that people defined by our erotic desires are being summoned into the church to help the church reunderstand what it is. In the process the tradition will get refashioned. Why not? It's gotten refashioned in every generation in one way or another. Probably in the process the solutions we come up with will be somebody's problem a hundred years from now, but I don't think we can avoid that. All we can do is live as honestly and with as much faithfulness to the gospel as we know how in our own time. We are presumably not the last group that will need to rebuild the church before it will have room for everyone. There will be others in the future. We may even, at some point, take on the role of resisting God's call to them, though I pray we will not. In any case, this is not about getting everything eternally *right*. It's about being faithful here and now.

M. R.: GOD'S FLAMING LAUGHTER

The Gospel as Subversion or the Gospel as Camp?

For several years, in teaching about gay spirituality, I used "The Gospel as Subversion" as one of my topics. The title was all too accurate: the gospel began, slowly but irresistibly, to subvert me and my vision of what gay spirituality must embody when it brings itself fully into the church. I began working on this idea quite seriously, speaking of the ways in which the gospel turns common sense upside down and upsets the most scrupulous dealer by slipping an extra joker in the deck. The very fact that my mind began to run to images of that sort, rather than to more staid and traditional ones, is almost proof enough of what happens when the gospel is turned loose in the worlds of gay culture. It begins to develop a life of its own, nudges you slyly and seizes you by the scruff of the mind (much as the parables of Jesus do), leaving you with that delighted and slightly ridiculous feeling you generally get when you are right in the middle of falling in love. Something strange is going on, but you haven't got the heart to change it back.

"The Gospel as Subversion" changed slowly to "The Gospel as Camp," or perhaps even "Who Says God Doesn't Flame?" Actually, it began to shift as I started looking at what subversion really is, and on how we gay men and lesbians have learned to use humor of a particular kind—the kind we call camp—to do it. It began to strike me as very arresting indeed that I attended endless classes, workshops, and retreats that looked at every aspect of gay spirit except what was actually happening in the breaks between sessions. As serious as our mutual exploration of Christianity and spirituality was, it dissolved into laughter regularly, almost irresistibly, as soon as a session ended (and often in the midst of it). Gay and lesbian culture was happening in the jokes, and it was utterly subversive of all the false piousness with which most churches have mishandled our sexuality.

What really began to make this notion gel was an image that appeared in the press during the Episcopal Church's General Convention several years ago, when the debates on gender and gay issues were in full swing.

An unfortunate photograph taken in the House of Bishops depicted three of the most violently anti-gay defenders of the faith seated in a row. They had been assuring their colleagues that they truly did love the sinner; engraved on their faces, however, were three identical Medusa-like glares that looked as if they had been set in concrete, defying anyone to believe that any quiver of life could ever pass those features. My first reaction, sane to the core, was a gut-knotting spasm of fear and anger: I know irrational hatred when I see it. But almost immediately on its heels came a reaction that was purely and definitely queer to the core: I couldn't help noticing that one of the three bishops bore a startling resemblance to an unusually peevish chicken (and there is probably nothing in nature that can look quite so peevish). I clipped it out of the paper, wrote, "And you'll know they're Christians by their love," and sent it to one of my friends, a gay priest.

And yes, that bit of humor is one of the most subversive things I can imagine: I can't do a great deal about bishops within the structure of the church, but minority groups learned long ago that this sort of humor serves several very healthy purposes. First, it delivers us from the sense that we are helpless in the face of irrational hatred and the abuse of power, restoring our sense of proportion. We are not really such dreadful people as they say we are, and they are a great deal more ridiculous than they know.

At this same convention, a number of gay and lesbian friends of mine managed to have a great old time, tension and all. Their humor did not deny the seriousness of the issues that are dividing congregations and dioceses, but they refused to give those issues the power to have the final word. And this, perhaps, is one of the most undervalued gifts we bring to the church.

The Humor-Impaired Christian

Too many Christians are humor impaired. This is not just a problem for Christians. This is a problem that people get from the attitude that says, "If it's religious, it has to be serious. God forbid that you should ever crack a smile. Worse yet, God forbid that *God* should ever crack a smile!"

I remember in my early childhood, when we'd visit the Reformed Church my grandparents attended, there were several elderly women who treated children as if they were dangerous little barbarians (yes, well, they may have had a point) who had to be severely repressed at all times. They wanted to make sure that there was as little childhood as possible and that it never intruded into the services of the church. Oddly enough, their facial expressions were exactly like those three bishops'. They were determined that no undisciplined stir of life would ever occur. The message was: don't wiggle, don't make any noise, sit still, don't pass notes, and above all, don't giggle. The idea of enjoying yourself in church was just marginally shy of papism, mass murder, and blasphemy.

It's small wonder that many of us still have a strong suspicion that, when we're looking at religious topics, we really ought to be quite serious about them. Consider, for example, the fact that the Bible is so miserably read in churches. All elements of life and humor (of which there are many in both the Old and New Testaments) are flattened out, or read in a self-conscious style midway between Eric Severeid and a Fireside Chat with FDR. I remember sitting in a bar watching a gay comedian do an old-time preacher routine in which, having removed his dentures and donned a clerical collar, he began reading the story of Jacob and Esau from a large black Bible. The gay audience erupted in gales of laughter when he got to the line, "Now, Esau was an hairy man [delicious shudder], but Jacob [sigh]—Jacob was a *smy-oo-ooth* man."

Too many of us remember that most of our Bible reading as youngsters consisted of finding the sexy parts and that we had (and have) our suspicions about David and Jonathan, not to mention Judith and her maid. In my teens, when I noticed that Mary Magdalene was not "Mary, Some Guy's Wife" or "Mary, Some Other Guy's Mother," but simply "Mary from Magdala," my dykely little heart rejoiced. I figured if Jesus had lived in this century, she'd still have followed him—on a motorcycle.

I know, this will seem somewhat over-the-top for non-gay Christians. I could, however, say it in any gay workshop, and I would be understood without anyone imagining that I was trying to subvert the gospel. I would be using the gospel to subvert the rigid assumptions of heterosexual culture.

All of this becomes worse when we turn to the gospel on the assumption that if Jesus said it, it must be terribly serious. After all, he was crucified, wasn't he? (And that, looked at through gay eyes, makes about as much sense as saying that you should always be very grim because, after all, you're going to die some day.) I often think Jesus must be scratching his head and thinking, "Why aren't they smiling?" A great deal of the gospel was really about poking at people's rigid and fixed religious assumptions.

The religious world of the first century was quite tidy, in theory. You knew who would grow up to be a priest, you knew who was going to be accepted in the house of Israel, you knew what your role was going to be, and therefore you knew how close you were to God. And because it was a relatively tidy religious scheme, some people were of course closer to God than others, which really had to do with how close you could be to the center of the Temple. Certain people were decidedly not as holy as others: prostitutes, divorced women (a priest could not marry one), tax collectors, Gentiles. Yet consistently, Jesus knocked over the walls and had the prostitutes and tax collectors dancing merrily into the kingdom of heaven. He was criticized because his followers had altogether too much fun, drinking wine and partying while the religious establishment, like the bishops in the picture, were being properly serious about the whole thing. God forbid that any of those walls should be breached. Yet over and over again, that's precisely what the gospel does: it subverts people's structured awareness and turns it on its head. I have a feeling that, given the choice between camp humor and a Jerry Falwell sermon, Jesus would have gone for the laughter any day.

Laughter as Subversion

Humor, as most marginalized groups learn sooner or later, is among the most deadly subversive activities on earth. It is one of the things that establishments truly cannot stand. And for that reason alone, it can serve as a powerful weapon in the battle to achieve self-esteem in the face of prejudice. I think of the time back before Stonewall, a time when police had no qualms about raiding bars and harassing and humiliating gay people, with no thought it would even be possible to fight back. Yet there was something about Gerri, a diminutive little queen, watching a mean-faced cop swagger into the bar with his nightstick prominently displayed, sighing and saying softly, "Well, here comes Little Alice Blue Gown again." I, an eighteen-year-old baby butch who still had an exaggerated fear of being arrested, invariably felt humiliated by the reminders that the Law apparently regarded me as a form of vermin not quite as respectable as the common cockroach. Gerri's sly little dig reminded me that the cop did, in fact, look pretty silly, as if he were imitating someone in an old Jimmy-Cagney-plays-Alcatraz film. The cop's own fear suddenly became apparent, and my own fear subsided.

It is not simply the oppressing establishment that becomes the target of gay humor: the religious world comes in for its share, as well, and most gay men and lesbians have heard all the jokes: "Never play chess with a Catholic. They can't tell the difference between a bishop and a queen." Or having been complimented on his new surplice, the server says, "Darling, it's not a surplice: it's a statement." The head of the altar guild might be a tad upset, but ask yourself why it is that that's the natural way we relate to each other even in a religious setting, and is one of the things that we try very hard not to let our fellow church members see. Yet I'm convinced that it's part of why much of the establishment is terrified of the gay and lesbian community, and at the same time is precisely why God wants us here.

This isn't just about making others look ridiculous, by the way, it's often about being able to pop the Monster Bubble of tension and reduce it to normal size again. Take, for example, the story from the Canadian Anglican Church's General Synod, which was being held in very hot weather in an old-fashioned, un-air-conditioned hall at McGill University. On the night before the Synod opened, the people who were setting up the booth for Integrity (the Anglican association for gay men and lesbians) had a brilliant idea. They rushed out to the local Chinatown and purchased five hundred Chinese fans, and affixed little labels that said, "I'm a Fan of Integrity." The anti-gay folks from the head table rushed over to the Integrity booth and grabbed a handful of fans. To Integrity's delight, the evening news coverage showed the most vocal of the anti-gay delegates holding forth, all the while fanning himself, with the "I'm a Fan of Integrity" label clearly visible

The Myth of the Natural Way of Life

Subversion is the ability to turn the world upside down, the ability to recognize when the emperor is naked. But it also has some dimensions that we need to explore at a deeper level.

Since gay men and lesbians are frequently accused of being unnatural, or at least of having unnatural appetites, it delights me to point out that *human beings have no single natural way of life*. It simply doesn't exist. All other creatures have a natural way of life, that is, one that is natural to them. Foxes are born as cubs and they grow up to be foxes. They don't have agonizing identity decisions to make. They know by the time they are little foxlings what their life's work is going to be: get out and chase chickens, eat chickens. They do not have to debate whether to remain carnivores or become vegetarians. Little tigers grow up to be big tigers: they live, hunt, mate, and parent exactly as tigers have always done.

This is not true of human beings. We are not equipped by instinct to be much of anything. Babies don't really know if they're human beings or pop-up toasters at first; it takes them a fair amount of time to figure out what is part of their own body and what isn't. It takes a huge amount of time for baby humans to become adult humans, and they can't do it by instinct alone.

We have to be acculturated in order to know how to live. And there is no natural way of life for us to embrace. There are no ways of life that are more natural than others; there are simply ways that are older or more familiar than others. It is no more natural for human beings to live in nuclear families than to live in extended families. It is no more natural for us to live by eating grains than it is to live by eating whale blubber. We eat what the environment provides. It is no more natural to spend our lives with ninety percent of our bodies covered with clothing than it is to spend most of our lives stark naked. Only after we'd begin to develop a surplus, a complex division of labor, could we begin to make real choices.

But here is the simple fact: all forms of human culture are equally invented. They are all products of the human imagination. They have nothing corresponding to them in nature. We are none of us natural in that sense.

It takes a long time to make the connections between the inside and the outside for human beings. We have to be acculturated to speak the language of our group, to know how to behave toward parents, younger brothers, strangers, and enemies. We are acculturated to regard small feet or large breasts or eyes of a certain color as attractive, and other features as unattractive. None of these are beautiful or ugly in and of themselves.

Only when we have mastered a certain number of the acculturated skills can we begin to connect our cultures with inner realities. And understand this quite clearly: human beings are a great deal more variable than the cultures in which they live. No cultural construct will fit every member of a society, no matter how carefully they are instructed or indoctrinated in the culture's assumptions. Some of us are born gay, and the fact is that most cultures are *(a)* too preoccupied with survival to encourage sexual activity that doesn't produce offspring, and *(b)* most are not sophisticated enough to recognize that multiple lifestyles can and do exist side by side. That only happens in a situation like ours when the predominant patterns of culture are disintegrating.

In Praise of Disintegration

It is not entirely reassuring to many people to realize that since all lifestyles are inventions, they are not only all equally natural, but equally *unnatural.* The only constant is the fact that, once having embraced a lifestyle, we become convinced that it is the only normal, sane, and decent way to live. All other ways become suspect. When a system is working (that is, when it is a reasonable match for the conditions of life experienced by most people), people regard it as obvious that it is not only the proper way to live, but that it should be eternal, universal, and sacrosanct.

When the cultural lens through which we are looking no longer matches the world we are viewing through it, people begin to question received wisdom, challenge the previously sacred, and begin pressing for a new definition of values, morality, and that most elusive of all things, "the truth." We happen to live in one of those periods of disintegration. Jesus happened to have lived in another. The end of what we call classical antiquity was also a time of enormous cultural shifts, a time when smaller, local belief systems found themselves being breached or over-whelmed by larger systems that were quite foreign at first.

Typically, what happens at times like that is that a tremendous amount of energy is released by those parts of the culture that were never successfully incorporated or assimilated in the prevailing world view. In other words, the fringes begin to destabilize the center of the culture. Toward the end of the Middle Ages, for instance, the emerging middle class, having no place in the existing four-class traditional society, became the source of agitation, destabilization, and reform. The fringes are often in violent collision with the forces that represent the former status quo and are fairly often identified as the source of all society's problems. This will sound fairly familiar to gay and lesbian Christians, who are "responsible" for the collapse of the American family, the deterioration of American religion, and the excesses of heterosexual lust that occurs in big-budget films and prime-time television. Don't ask me to explain this last: it merely demonstrates that even the most intelligent human beings can be subject to outbursts of terminal silliness.

The fringes, once they move to center stage, begin to rigidify in turn, and develop a tremendous stake in maintaining the new balance. Eventually, some other group will take its place at the fringe, to serve as the challenge and the destabilizer. Obviously, in this century, the gay and lesbian community is one of the big destabilizers. There is an element of truth in the suspicion that many conservative people have, that something very threatening is happening to their world. It is. But it's not coming from where they think it is, and the remedy is not what they think it is. The unfortunate thing is that this kind of destabilization and re-formation will not happen in less than two hundred years, which means most of us will not be around to benefit from it.

Tying It All Together

To return to the notion of camp, and its function as a subversive force, it also functions on the fringes, with exactly the kind of energy I spoke of earlier. And energy is the basis of all creativity.

Jesus does not seem to have called the people who were comfortable and successful in the heart of the establishment. Those he called were at the fringes in many ways: women who didn't stay at home, fishermen who had no claims to religious authority, despised tax collectors, demon-possessed women who weren't properly identified with a respectable father, husband, or son. Did Jesus recognize that only people on the fringes can remake the center? Do we recognize that our being on the fringes makes us one of the forces to remake the center?

And one of the groups to help remake the church? The thought is both terrifying and just a bit outrageous.

What, after all, is so outrageous about camp? For one thing, it deliberately crosses lines and confounds categories. Playing on the words "bishop" and "queen," for instance, places the most formidable of religious authorities in the same category with Auntie Robert at the neighborhood bar. And yes, gay men and women *do* cross lines.

The religious world that Jesus belonged to assigned everything to certain boundaries. The things that are called abominations, unclean, and so on, were all characterized by the fact that they crossed boundaries. The implication was, "Okay, this is an animal that chews a cud and has a divided hoof. It's a proper cow. It's clean and you can eat it. But wait a minute, here's another animal that has a divided hoof, but it doesn't chew a cud. It's a pig, and therefore not a proper cow at all, so it's unclean, and you can't eat it." Its only crime, the thing that makes it an abomination, and renders it unclean, is that it doesn't fit perfectly inside the boundaries of the category.

This is part of what happens to gay men and lesbians. If your category is man, you're supposed to father children by a woman; if you're a woman, you're supposed to have children. What about those of us who cross the lines? It's as if Father Abraham decides that Mother Sarah isn't his type and goes off into the sunset with Larry the Lifeguard, while Mother Sarah dumps the kids on her in-laws, buys a Harley, and moves to the Russian River with her personal trainer, Lisa.

That paragraph, by the way, is a fairly good example of camp humor. It rests on bringing together incompatible elements (the most impressive patriarch and matriarch in the Old Testament and what my friend Cyr calls the interchangeable *nouveau-gaie*, who arrive in California by the droves from Arkansas and South Dakota). That is exactly what gay humor is about, and that is exactly what makes it so scary to straight culture. It takes the cultural ideal of manliness, dresses it up in black leather with millions of zippers, and explodes the category by cutting out the seat of the black leather pants so that passersby can see the pink long johns peeking through.

"Darling, this isn't a surplice, it's a statement." I happen to know the man who said that, and he is perfectly serious about his work as a worship assistant and a lay eucharistic minister. He stands as a reminder that faith and laughter do not have to avoid contact.

Let me offer a final image of the function of gay humor. It works best in those areas where people get frozen into their boxes, and become too rigid to change without breaking. It's exactly like what happens along the faults in earthquake country. The tectonic plates slip against each other and create vast amounts of tension. If the plates can release that tension, you don't have an earthquake. When the plates cannot release the tension, the pressure builds up to a point at which only a massive earthquake can relieve it.

The words hold an intimate connection between spirit, spiritual, and spirited, that we have forgotten. It's time we took our spirited laughter into the church and to the discussion table, instead of confining gay spirit to the lobby at break times. The church needs this of us, lest it die of its own seriousness.

Flaming, Flaming God

God flames like a drag queen on Gay Hallowe'en, gesturing at the world and saying, "Just look at the extravaganza I've created! Look at the delicious variety of men and women I've dreamed up. And look at the way I keep shifting the lines around just when you think you have it all taped down."

God's laughter is at the heart of life, in God's delight in mixing up the categories, breaking down the walls, and generally pulling the rug out from under us when we begin to take ourselves too seriously. Especially when we begin to mistake our own prejudices for the voice of God.

What dances underneath gay humor is the laughter of God, the laughter that we hear in the gospel. We hear the story of the vineyard owner and are irresistibly drawn into a wry acknowledgment of our own expectations and failings. There they are, the spiritual overachievers, wearing their correct little harvest suits, trying to look eager and reliable, and lined up at the first hour to make sure they'll get hired for the job. They assume that God is as impressed with them as they are with themselves. But then comes the joke: at the eleventh hour, two drag queens drift in (or, rather, they make an entrance), gorgeously and unsuitably attired for the field, having spent the day trying on shoes, and go out and put in twenty-seven minutes (less time for a latté break).

And there is something that delights the heart when we think of all those little eager beavers in their harvest suits lining up for the payoff and discovering that they have to stand in line with these two fabulous creatures and don't get a single cent more.

Let me be a little more camp yet about this: it gives my heart great delight to think that perhaps when we get to God's banquet, those three bishops will discover that God has put them at a table with me. Or better yet, has assigned them to wait on it.

BILL: GRACE AS SURPRISE

Jesus' Good News

Remember that gospel means "good news." To be sure, we've divorced the word so far from its history that we seldom think of it in those terms. I've even heard people use the word gospel as if it meant some sort of law: This is gospel; so you must do as I tell you now. I've heard other people use it to mean something like "least bad news": God is angry and punitive and doesn't like you much but has left this little loophole that you might be able to squeeze through if you work at it very hard. But the gospel of the New Testament is just what it says: good news. So, whatever you hear, if it's not news and it's not good, then it's not gospel. If it's the same old yammering and it doesn't create any new life or new opportunity for reflection or understanding, then it's not gospel. Even if what you hear is news to you, if it's not *good* news, in some important way, it's still not gospel.

That doesn't mean that it will always be obvious from the start that it's good news. Our experience often corresponds to that embarrassed and half-conscious prayer: "God, thank you for surprising us with grace. And please don't do it again." Grace, at the beginning, may seem overwhelming, destabilizing, perplexing. We may have little idea what to do with it at first. A good deal of Jesus' teaching proceeds in exactly that way. Think, for example, about the familiar parable that we usually call The Prodigal Son (Luke 15:11–32). That's not really a very good name for it, is it? The characters of the father and the older son are at least as important as the younger son, the prodigal. I heard someone suggest a few years back that it ought to be called The Prodigal Father, because the father doesn't behave properly in this parable at all. A good patriarch of the ancient Mediterranean world was supposed to be staid and severe and demanding. The ancient Roman ideal was that an adult male of good family and social standing would always look, in public, as much as possible like a statue, something on the order of those Medusa-like bishops M. R. mentioned. (Too bad if you looked like a chicken—you would then look like the statue of a chicken.)

This father doesn't behave correctly at all. When he sees the younger son coming, he takes the mere act of return as sufficient. The son has carefully worked out a little speech of repentance, but he never gets to deliver it. His father doesn't give him a chance. It must have been a bit of a disappointment for the boy. But the father rushes out—exactly what he should not be doing—hugs him, dirty and smelly as he must have been, and tells the servants to bring out the best robe, bring out a ring, kill the fatted calf. Clearly, we're going to have a party.

But the parable ends with the elder brother; he's the person we're left with when it's over. And the elder brother is in the right—there's no question about that. He's worked hard at being in the right, like those other good doobies, the ones who got hired first in the Parable of the Laborers in the Vineyard (Matthew 20:1–16). They were in the vineyard working hard all day, and they were angry when the people who'd only worked one hour were paid the same as they. They were in the right, too. The elder brother, then, is justified when he complains about the attention given to his prodigal brother, and the father really never questions that. Instead, he says, "Look, everything I've got is yours. But your younger brother is back from the dead, so what else are we supposed to do?" Still, at the end of the parable, you never find out what the elder brother did. Did he stand outside and sulk or did he go inside and join the party—or maybe go inside and sulk, to be the wet blanket of the occasion?

Jesus never tells us. He just leaves the listeners hanging with a set of questions. Whom, in the story, do you understand? Whom are you most like? Are you like the prodigal son? Sure, we can all relate to him in one way or another probably. The elder brother? Yes, probably we can all relate to him, too. Or are you like the father? Could you be that generous? Probably all of us, at some time in our lives, could relate to him also. What the story really winds up doing is breaking up our existing expectations, pushing us to rearrange our presuppositions. There are no neat solutions here.

Or take another of Jesus' stories, The Good Samaritan (Luke 10:25–37). We've reduced this one to a kind of ethical platitude now: it's nice to be nice. What are you supposed to do? You're supposed to help the person who needs your help. But that's really not how it's told in Luke. The scene is set when a lawyer asks Jesus a tricky question: What is the most important commandment in the law? And Jesus turns the question back on him and says "Well, what do you think?" In Matthew and Mark, it's Jesus who gives us the summary of the law, but in Luke's Gospel, it's the lawyer who names the two central commandments—to love God with your whole self and to love your neighbor as you love yourself. (Incidentally, I think that does imply a commandment to love yourself, which has tended to get suppressed, at least in the teaching I grew up with. But the truth came clear for me when a student preacher at Good

Shepherd read this text and said, "You know, I look around at us all and I think if we were to love our neighbors as we love ourselves, God help our neighbors.")

But then the lawyer has another question, Luke tells us he is "wanting to justify himself." The question is "So who is my neighbor?" Who is it that I'm responsible for loving the way that I love myself? The lawyer is a bit like the good doobies at the beginning of the day in the market-place. He's a bit like the older brother. He's in the right. He wants to stay in the right and to know that he's in the right. All this seems perfectly reasonable. But Jesus tells him the story about the good Samaritan.

You know the story: a Jewish man from Jerusalem is traveling down to Jericho. He gets mugged on the way and left for dead. A priest from the Temple at Jerusalem comes by, and he moves to the far side of the road in order to skirt around the man lying there. Now a priest was a sacred person, and one thing that he had to avoid was contact with the dead, because it would disqualify him for a longish period of time from service in the Temple. So the priest plays it safe. Next there comes a Levite, also a Temple official. He's not quite as sacred as the priest, but he's also involved in the Temple service. He doesn't want to take the chance of being defiled by a corpse, either. And then along comes—who?

Well, simple, popular tales, like Jesus' parables, often abide by the "rule of three," and the third person should be someone who represents the next step down in the same hierarchy. My favorite folk tales, as the youngest in my family, were the ones where the youngest son was the third person and got things right after his older brothers had messed up. So, according to the rule of three, the next person down the hierarchy of sacredness after the priest and the Levite would be a lay Israelite. The early audience would expect that a lay Israelite would be the hero. But no! Along comes a Samaritan. Now, we have to fill that in with some mod-ern equivalent. Think of somebody who's the hereditary enemy of your folk, someone of whom you're so suspicious that you wouldn't even want to eat a meal with him, the sort of person you detest before you've even met him. If you're a modern Israeli, this person is a Palestinian. If you're a Palestinian, this person is an Israeli. And this is the person who stops and takes care of the man who's been beaten up!

At the end of the story, Jesus asks a question, but it's not the question we usually think. He doesn't ask, "Who behaved like a neighbor here?" or "Who treated the man who'd been mugged as a neighbor?" He asks, "Who turned out to *be* neighbor to the man who had fallen among thieves?" The lawyer responds—he can't bring himself to say "the Samaritan"—he says, "the one who took care of him." That's not what we usually take the story to mean. It doesn't say, "You're supposed to be like the good Samaritan and treat everyone as your neighbor." It says, "This is how you get to be somebody's neighbor." Don't wait for some rule to tell you who you're bound to and who you're not. Create your own neighbors. The story starts in the lawyer's world, but it ends up in a different world altogether. Not a world where you justify yourself by living according to the rules, but a world where you're enlarging the rules, opening them up, making a new world that's bigger and more generous than the one you thought you were living in.

So the parables of Jesus seem to be told with the intention of shaking up your presuppositions, of trying to put you off the world you thought you knew just enough that you have to start formulating a new one. After hearing The Prodigal Son you don't really want to be the prodigal son, but you don't want to be the older brother, either. And if you're like me, you think, "Well, I don't think I can be the father. I'm just not that generous. So where do I belong in the story? Maybe I have to rewrite myself in order to rewrite the story. Maybe I have to think again about the world I'm living in." And the story of the good Samaritan leaves me with my question reversed. Not "To whom am I responsible?" but "How can I create neighbors? How can I become somebody else's neighbor?"

Coming Out as Good News

I think all this is very much like the way the coming-out process works for those of us who are lesbians or gay men. You're finally able to say to yourself—whether soon or late—"I'm a gay man" or "I'm a lesbian. I belong to that group I've been taught to be suspicious of, to avoid, to think are bad people." As somebody put it back in the Stonewall era, "We are the people our parents warned us against." When you come to that moment of discovery, your whole world is broken open, and you're not given an automatic replacement for it. Coming out may be a little easier now than it was twenty years ago, at least for those of us lucky enough to be born into the right family or town or church. But even now, you're not going to be given an automatic replacement for the world you've just seen break apart. Some people who don't know us very well think there's a clearly defined alternative, something called "the gay lifestyle." There are a lot of gay people in this world, but there isn't a gay lifestyle. Gay people differ from one another just as much as heterosexual people differ from one another. What sets us apart is simply the society's decision that we're strange and different and maybe just shouldn't exist. So when we come out, we find our worlds shaken up, broken apart, and our old presuppositions called into question, and we have to begin again. This is a moment of great surprise, great opportunity, great grace.

When you're surprised by grace in this particular fashion, it doesn't always feel like good news at first. It may feel like the exact opposite of good news, in fact. It may be only bit by bit that you discover that it really is good news, that it's grace. For myself I think I began discovering that with the realization that suddenly all sorts of energy was available to me intellectually and emotionally, energy that had apparently been tied up for years and years in not noticing, not dealing with what was perfectly obvious. A lot of my old friends had known for years that I was gay. It's a fairly common experience, actually—coming out to old friends who say, "Oh, yeah, well, I always kind of thought so . . . " and you think, "Yeah, well, why didn't you tell me?" But of course, I wouldn't have listened if they had.

So the good news, the surprise of grace, isn't always something that's easy for us to accept or even to recognize in the beginning. On top of that, we may also have a lot of inner resistance to it. If you've spent your whole life thinking that God is the great police clerk in the sky, checking off your misdeeds, major and minor, then it's going to be very difficult to think of God instead as the father of the prodigal son who's so excited to see his wayward child again that he doesn't wait for the apology that he must have known was coming. Instead, he not only welcomes his son back, but celebrates his return to life. That kind of God can be very difficult to believe in, because we've got so much invested in a very different picture of God.

I know a gay man who was quite closed off from the church. Like many of us, he had been burned very badly by the church of his childhood and youth. He came a few times to Good Shepherd and heard the kind of gospel there that this book is trying to convey. His own background was Methodist, so high-church Anglicanism probably seemed a little strange to him. But, more important than that, he just couldn't bring himself to think that the Christianity being preached there was quite the real article. It was just too friendly. Now, actually Good Shepherd is pretty mainstream, when it comes right down to it. I've heard more serious preaching on the doctrines of the Trinity and the Incarnation there than anyplace else I've ever gone to church.

We don't cross-examine people to see how orthodox they are, because we don't look at orthodoxy as a kind of boundary that you've got to stay inside. We think of it more as a resource. The doctrine of the Trinity has turned out to be a great resource for us, since it talks about reality being, at its very roots, social, and founded on love—the kind of love that can't not give itself, and which therefore has to create community so that love can be shared. Trinity Sunday is an occasion I've actually begun to look forward to, whereas most of my life it's been something to dread because you could expect the sermon to be terribly intellectual and evasive because it was assumed that the Trinity couldn't have anything to do with ordinary life. So actually Good Shepherd can be quite conventional, theologically. The great difference is that it's actually focused not on theology, but on the surprise of grace. So it seemed odd to me that my friend couldn't quite imagine that Good Shepherd was real Christianity.

But what was the problem really about? I think it was something that a lot of us experience. Having experienced religion as homophobic, we go on to identify God as homophobic. A God who isn't homophobic won't seem real to us. Religion encourages that. It isn't God, but it wants to be. That's why idolatry is such a big and important sin in Scripture. It isn't some sin that only people who have strange images in their temples commit. It's the central temptation of *all* religious people. We *want* religion to be God, because then we'll have a God that's safely inside this world, that we can relegate to Sunday morning, that we can sum up in a series of things you have to believe, and things you have to do, that we can control through rites. That's the kind of God we would rather have, because the real God, who plays these jokes called "grace" on us—the real God is very big and scary no matter how loving, no matter how prodigal in generosity, no matter how determined to welcome us back into the family. (It's God, after all, who has to do the welcoming, not the church.) No matter how good that God is, that God is still big and scary and unpredictable.

So there is a part of each of us that would rather have the idolatrous religion, the kind of religion we can rely on to stay put. We'd rather have a religion that rejects us than have the real God who might love us in unexpected ways. That image of homophobic church and homophobic God is part of the internalized homophobia that sticks with us long after we come out, that we shed only bit by bit in the course of many years. We are still apt to encounter it in unexpected ways long after we thought we had gotten rid of it. Even after we've gotten over thinking we're *bad*, it still may tell us that we're not as *good* as other people. We think we can't expect to be treated the same as other people. We think that we're the "problem," instead of recognizing that other people happen to have a problem in relationship to us. It's very easy for homophobia to creep back in, especially in situations where we don't feel quite at ease, where we may even be in real danger—if not of life and limb, then at least of livelihood. There are times when, to be practical, we have to be really cautious. But every time we have to do that it reinforces that inner sense of being not quite worthy, not quite as good as others, not quite safe in this world.

This is exactly what we need to get away from, what we need to be delivered from. And yet, at the same time, it's familiar; and it's often easier to live in the familiar world, even if it's a nasty one, than in the unfamiliar world that you don't know yet. "Better the devil I know than the devil I don't know." The possibility that that unfamiliar world might be inhabited, not by devils, but by God, is very hard to rely on when you haven't been there yet, or at least haven't lived in it for very long at a stretch.

Returning from Exile

Now that's not just a problem for gay and lesbian people; it's a problem for people. When I have taught spirituality courses in the past I've often used a book by John Fortunato called *Embracing the Exile*. It's a book about coming out, about embracing that scary world where everything is not safely in place—a world where you can breathe more freely, but not a predictable world. And one of the surprises for me, in teaching with that particular book, is that many heterosexual students, when they read the book, will say, "You know, this is about my experience, too." A larger world inhabited by a loving God is a world that other people long for, too.

Almost all of us have been made to feel at some point in our lives as if we don't measure up, as if we don't truly belong, as if God must love everybody else but probably not us. That's part of why we find it easy to misread the second part of the Summary of the Law. It says very plainly, "Love your neighbor as yourself." It doesn't say, "Love your neighbor instead of yourself," though I think that's how most of us have heard it. It doesn't even say, "Love your neighbor more than yourself." It says, "Love your neighbor as yourself." Well, if that's the standard, then it might be a good thing to love yourself a bit, if only because it might improve the way you deal with your neighbor. It would be an act of generosity, wouldn't it? But we don't usually read it that way. We read it as a way of saying, "You're not important. Your neighbor's the person who's important."

A wonderful poem by George Herbert sums up for me the difficulty of accepting the surprise of grace. It's the third poem in *The Temple* that bears the name "Love," and it's the final, climactic poem in the central part of the book. I think it represents for Herbert the goal for Christian life and experience. The poem is a dialogue between Love as the host and the poet as the guest:

> Love bade me welcome, yet my soul drew back,
> Guilty of dust and sin.
> But quick-ey'd Love, observing me grow slack
> From my first entrance in,
> Drew nearer to me, sweetly questioning
> If I lack'd anything.
>
> "A guest," I answer'd, "worthy to be here";
> Love said, "You shall be he."
> "I, the unkind, ungrateful? ah my dear,
> I cannot look on thee."
> Love took my hand and smiling did reply,
> "Who made the eyes but I?"

"Truth, Lord, but I have marr'd them; let my shame
   Go where it doth deserve."
"And know you not," says Love, "who bore the blame?"
   "My dear, then I will serve."
"You must sit down," says Love, "and taste my meat."
   So I did sit and eat.

What a terrible struggle to get to that point of surrendering to one's own joy. What a terrible struggle to get to the point of actually accepting the invitation. It's not easy. It's not just gay and lesbian people who find it difficult. It's people who find it difficult.

In a sense, gay and lesbian people are better off—yes, it can happen—but only because we've got the problem laid out so clearly for us. Sometimes it's easier to deal with a problem in a more exaggerated form because you're pretty sure what it is. Fortunato's book proved to be helpful for heterosexual students because he was dealing with a more extreme expression of a common human problem—where people have been told over and over again in very plain, if not always overt or explicit ways, that they're not acceptable. We who are lesbian or gay know where the problem lies; we can name it or describe it. And therefore we have something that's a little easier to recognize. That can make our experience a helpful model, a kind of key that can unlock other people's experience where it hasn't been clear, where a vaguer feeling of being unacceptable, of not being quite right, of not being full members of the family has dogged people.

And so grace takes us by surprise and calls us and invites us in. It tells us, in the words of Henry Vaughan, that faith has "of a private family made open house." And, still, once we work up the courage to set foot inside the door, we may find ourselves hanging back and thinking, "Oh, but we're not really meant to sit at the table." And again grace comes to us in the form of God's love, in the form of the God who is love, and takes us by the hand and says, "What's your problem? I've taken care of that already. What! you want to wait on table? No, you're my guest. You've got to come sit at table and enjoy the feast."

Once we become adults, it's often very difficult for us to accept gifts. It's easier sometimes to give them than to accept them. When you're giving them you can feel that you're in control. When you're accepting them, who knows what might happen? You might have to just give up and let yourself be loved. Being loved is the biggest surprise grace has in store for us, I think, and it seems we keep having to be surprised by it over and over again. We may even accept it for a bit and live in that ecstasy for a little while, and then we go back to our old ways of thinking they couldn't have meant *us*. So we try to earn it, try to deserve it. And those of us who feel we've started from further back in the race assume that we have to run even faster. There are plenty of jokes about gay men and the amount of time we have spent in our lives trying to be the best little boys in the world, because we knew somewhere deep down, early on, even if we didn't know we were gay, that we had a lot to make up for, and we'd better get busy on it real soon. That, of course, is what makes us such excellent interior decorators and why we form the fashion police of the world. Uh-huh.

The Timetable of Grace

There's another thing about grace. Not only is it a gift (and all we can do is accept it), and not only does it threaten to change our world in unpredictable ways—all that's scary in itself—but, worse yet, grace is on its own peculiar timetable, and it will always be on its own peculiar timetable. We never know how long we're going to have to live in the vale of tears or the forest of frustration, unable to find our way out of it. There's no telling about that. Grace comes when grace comes. The moment of reassurance comes when God senses that we're finally ready to comprehend what it's about. Henry Vaughan, who wrote the poem about faith, endured a lot of frustration on that score. I suspect he was of a somewhat depressive temperament, which can make hope more difficult, but also he lived in very difficult times. Nothing went right. He was not rewarded with moments when his world was behaving the way that he thought it should. It was the time of the Civil War and the Commonwealth in England, when everybody felt their world was upset, but most of all those people who were trying to be faithful to an ideal of Anglicanism.

Many of Vaughan's poems embody not so much a certainty about the goodness of God, as a kind of longing intensity that at some point God's goodness would make itself known. In a few of his poems the light does break through, and it's all the more powerful because you realize that this is running counter to his own temperament. One of his last poems "The Revival," begins with images of daybreak. Vaughan was apparently big on waking up early to greet the dawn and to greet God in the dawn. But then it shifts, and the imagery, instead of being daylight replacing dark, becomes that of a long-delayed spring bringing winter to an end. At the very end come two wonderful lines about grace making itself felt in the heart:

> Unfold! unfold! Take in His light,
> Who makes thy cares more short than night.
> The joys, which with His day-star rise,
> He deals to all but drowsy eyes;

And (what the men of this world miss)
Some drops and dews of future bliss.
   Hark! how his winds have changed their note,
And with warm whispers call thee out.
The frosts are past, the storms are gone,
And backward life at last comes on.
The lofty groves in express joys
Reply unto the turtle's voice;
And here in dust and dirt, O here
The lilies of His love appear!

Notice where we are at the end. Not in some perfect ethereal, spiritual world that's free of the body. Lilies have to grow in dust and dirt. Those lilies, incidentally, allude to the Song of Songs in the Old Testament. Doves and spices and lilies are always recurring in seventeenth-century poetry as allusions to God's love for us. The turtle's voice ("turtle" meaning "turtle-dove") is another allusion to the Song of Songs. But the storms are over, spring at last has arrived, and it's in the dust and dirt of our actual lives—not the perfect us that we would like to present to God on a Sunday morning, but the dust and dirt of our actual lives— that God's love becomes apparent.

    That's us. That's our lives—with lilies blooming in them, lilies that spring up when grace sees that it's the right moment for us, lilies that come as a big surprise no matter how many times we've been told that spring will come again and the lilies will bloom. Spring after spring, it is always good news, always a surprise. Always grace.

M. R.: THE GOD WHO LOVES SURPRISES

"I Created You . . ."

I suppose most of us have asked, at some time or another, "Why did God create gay men and lesbians?" Or more personally, "Why me, God?" The camp answer, of course, is "Just lucky, I guess." Even when we come to terms with having been created gay, and have come to be grateful that we are, the question remains. Why would God create gay men and lesbians?

I'm going to come at this question somewhat indirectly, on the assumption that sometimes it is the thing we see out of the corner of the eye that most arrests our attention, and that the answer to a maddeningly insoluble question often comes to us when we are looking at something else. This is straight out of my own spiritual journey, a story I heard from my teacher, André Fikri: a Sufi story, in fact. Perhaps it will let us hear things in a way that the very familiarity of Christianity obscures to us.

It's the story of a woman whose name was Mahmouda, who was born sometime late in the fourteenth century, probably in Anatolia. Mahmouda was born with severe handicaps: the left side of her body was not fully developed, so that her left leg was much shorter than the right leg, and her left arm never fully developed, so her hand had very little strength in it and could do very little. In the fourteenth century in a devout Muslim family, this was considered the true misfortune: she was an unmarriageable daughter. All the same, the family was devoutly religious and firmly believed that there was some reason this child had been born into their family and some purpose to her flaw. And though her body set her apart from other children, her mind and heart were alive and bright, and she herself seems to have been a cheerful little girl.

When she was twelve years old, the family went to visit relatives in a larger city and stayed with an uncle who was a potter. One day, as she was sitting there watching her uncle make a pot, her attention was seized by what she saw. He worked sitting on a bench, his left foot tucked up under him, while his right foot turned the wheel. He steadied

the mass of clay with his left hand while the strong right hand shaped
the pot. And suddenly she had an insight that would change her whole
life: here was a space in the world that was exactly the same shape as she
was. God, she understood, had made her for a purpose, and all she had
to do was consent to stepping into the space that had been prepared for
her. (It was a conviction she kept all her life.)

So Mahmouda learned to make pots and delighted in the fact that she
had no handicap there. She sat all day with the shorter left leg tucked
up under her, turning the wheel with her right foot, steadying the mass
with the weaker, less skilled left hand, while shaping it with the right
hand. Suddenly she was a full member of her family, someone who
added to the family's welfare. Now, her family did not make the best or
fanciest pottery in town. What they produced was probably the equivalent of what you'd find at a K-Mart: a nice serviceable pot for every-
day use. And that is what Mahmouda did for the next thirty years.

In those days, house, home, workshop, and store were all in the same
building. The family lived in the back, or upstairs; the front was the
workshop where the pots were made; and the front of the house
opened up to disclose a counter where buyers could come to inspect
the wares. She was sitting at the wheel making pots one day, with the
shutter opened onto the market square, the first time she saw a Mevlevi
dervish perform the Turn, the dance movement that has earned the
Mevlevis the inaccurate nickname of "whirling dervishes." It is not simply a dance, but a form of prayer, for prayer is one of the ways in which
we draw the life of God down into the world. She watched him turn,
right palm held open, facing upward to receive God's energy, and the
left palm facing downward to return that life into the world. She
understood this instantly, and for the first time in years, she felt
tremendous regret about her handicaps, for she realized she could
never pray in that way.

So she sat there continuing to turn the wheel and shape the clay, and
suddenly she recognized that she was in fact doing the same thing, that
she was drawing down the life of God into the world with every turn
of the wheel, with every motion of her hand. And an amazing thing
began to happen. People started to come from all over town to buy her
pots, because they had become so gorgeous. They were irresistible. They
had become things of utter beauty. And so she sat there, turning the
wheel, singing her prayers. She hadn't learned to read and write, so she
sang her prayers, as she made them with her hands. Presently people
would come and just sit nearby to listen to her as she spoke to God, and
eventually she gained the reputation of being a Holy Woman.

Students gathered around her, which is the typical pattern of Sufi
spirituality. Nobody tells you you're a teacher. You discover it when you
look around you and find you have students. It's also traditional that as

schools form, the students must support the teacher, and they will often build a place for the teacher, which is what her students did. They got a piece of property, and prepared a wonderful house with a fountain and a courtyard, and all these wonderful things in it, and proudly presented it to her. And the first thing she did was to move her potter's wheel in and start making pots again. Her students were shocked and said, "No, no, no! Mahmouda, you don't understand. You don't have to make pots anymore. We're going to take care of you." She laughed at them and said, "No, no, no! You are the ones who don't understand. The moment I understood who God was, I never *had* to make another pot."

The most beguiling story about her is one that she told at the very end of her life, only a few months before she died in her nineties (which in the fourteenth century was quite remarkable): She dreamed that she had died, and found herself at the entrance to Paradise. As a devout Muslim woman, she thought she had to first be judged to see whether she would be admitted to Paradise. So she stood waiting patiently and a little nervously at the entrance, until she noticed someone yelling and waving to her in the distance. It was God, running toward her with outstretched arms, shouting, "Mahmouda! Oh, Mahmouda! Welcome, welcome!" Mahmouda was startled as God embraced her and continued, "I've waited so long for this moment. I've been longing to see you, and here you are at last. Come in, come in and enjoy Paradise."

But Mahmouda asked, "But wait! Don't you have to judge me first? I know I've made so many mistakes, and I know I've failed so many times, and . . ."

But God wouldn't even let her finish. "Mahmouda! I made you little and weak and full of flaws. You have done so much more than I ever imagined you could do!"

Mahmouda exclaimed, "But—but—you're God! You're the All-Knowing. How could you not know everything I would do?"

With that, God looked around, beckoned to her to come closer, leaned over and whispered into her ear, "I'll tell you a secret, Mahmouda. I made the stars and the planets to obey me. And I made the angels and all the bright spirits to adore me. But you, Mahmouda—I made you to surprise me."

Tossing Aside the Blueprints

Odd as it sounds, this is a fitting subtext for this next area of exploration, which is an attempt to answer that original question, "What did God make us for?" I remember learning in catechism that God made us for some reason like praising and glorifying God forever. I have always felt it was vaguely blasphemous to suggest that God created humanity simply to provide a cheering section. Mahmouda's answer seems closer to the God Jesus reveals in the gospel than that.

Too often, when we talk about what God's purpose for us is, we have the idea that God has a master set of blueprints that (if we only knew what page our particular blueprint was on) would tell us once and for all what we are supposed to be. Worse, we have embraced too heartily the notion that God is so uninventive as to have devised only one blueprint and that every human being must therefore serve the same purpose.

This is fairly important for gay and lesbian Christians to understand, because the church often gives us the impression that just by virtue of not being heterosexuals we have somehow failed the reason for our creation. This is a long-standing tradition, of course, the notion that the only reason for sexuality is the creation of children (a teaching of dubious morality in a world where dangerous overpopulation condemns a large number of those children to lives of misery).

Whatever the Western religious tradition has said about it, gay men and lesbians have been reaching for answers, and beginning to find them for much longer than most of us know. A little history might be useful here. As someone who came out in the late fifties, I sometimes think that the most popular and accepted ideas nowadays seem to be a clear step backwards, whose net effect has been to render gay men and women as spiritually dead as their straight counterparts. But I tend to show the imprint of the fifties and sixties. In the fifties and early sixties, gay liberation as I came to know it had a strong and un-self-conscious spiritual face. In many ways, it fit into the category of "spiritual movement" in the same way that the counterculture of the sixties did.

It surprises many people to know that the pioneers in gay liberation were almost entirely disowned or forgotten by the next generation, whose agenda was primarily political and economic. The second generation referred to the first generation as "separatists"; the first labeled the second "assimilationists." We are a great deal more sophisticated now and more apt to divide along lines of "essentialists" and "constructionists," but neither is a cause to drink to, much less die for.

In the early part of this century, there were a number of very interesting ideas floating around, fostered by writers nobody bothers to read anymore, and people whose names and faces have gone the way of the Free Press, Peter Max, and the Fabulous Furry Freak Brothers. Some, earlier in the century, had some very extravagant claims to make about gay men and women, people like Edward Carpenter and Gerald Heard, who were convinced that there was a spiritual dimension to gay men and women that had a particular purpose in human culture and history.[2] Some of their ideas represent fairly extravagant claims, suggesting that gay and lesbian men and women represented a higher stage of psychic and sexual evolution than heterosexuals (and a comforting thought it was, too, back in 1963), or that gay and lesbian people were nature's way of educating the genders by bridging the gap between them.

While very few people would espouse these claims nowadays, it is more widely accepted that in cultures in which roles are rigidly gender-defined, gay men and lesbians are cast in roles that do, in fact, allow them to move between the two worlds of male and female. It is no accident that so many people who are attracted to art, music, dance, and other creative endeavors are often suspected of being gay (whether they are or not), and that religious enterprises seem to attract a disproportionate percentage of gay and lesbian people. This latter may simply be true in part because, for a number of centuries, the safest place for a gay man or lesbian was in a religious order, where no one would question a person's having opted out of mandatory heterosexual marriage. It was perfectly respectable and allowed individuals to live in a community that was exclusively male or exclusively female, and often to explore roles not acceptable for men or women in ordinary society. The Reformation was something of a disaster for gay men and women, narrowing the range of roles they could play by destroying the safe space of monastery and convent. The twentieth-century fixation on the nuclear family has narrowed the range even further.

Recarving a Space

The fact that fewer safe spaces exist in society, and that religion in particular seems unwilling to admit that gay men and lesbians can serve any positive role whatever in the church, makes it even more important to arrive at our own sense of definition, the recognition of purpose that in some ways may be as simple as Mahmouda's understanding that there was a hole of exactly her shape in the heart of things.

There are some fairly obvious roles that we can and do play, whether or not they are recognized as having value by the majority community. Because many of us do not create biological families, it means that we have to explore other dimensions of generativity, offering our commitment and care to a wider group of people. It is no longer any esoteric piece of knowledge that among many Native American nations, gay men and lesbians were designated to serve certain spiritual roles on behalf of the community *because* they weren't embedded in the welfare of a single clan or family in the same way. While less and less community can be found in large urban centers, this is not true of gay and lesbian neighborhoods. Gay and lesbian neighborhoods, whether the Castro or West Hollywood, are recognizably communities, in which people interact with each other and their environment in more accessible and less aggressive ways than is now the norm in the American city. In the church, too, gay and lesbian Christians are frequently the ones who add to the liturgical, musical, and artistic richness of the community, rather than just its functionality.

In part, these are skills gay men and lesbians learn early. Many of us simply have to create our own families, separate from our biological roots. We are forced to learn how this is done, which means that our social life rapidly expands from the simple matter of personal sexual gratification to the skills that reach out beyond the immediate "family" to the community.

In the highly privatized world of American religion, this is a lesson the mainstream churches could well learn from us, particularly when so many parishes are slowly dying because of their inability to reach out beyond themselves to welcome others of different races, languages, economic brackets, and lifestyles. Gay and lesbian communities go right across the full range of color, religion, gender, economics, and so on; it is no coincidence that the rainbow flag is an apt symbol of the gay community. This kind of community-building should be one of the tasks of Christian churches. The church should be the place where we learn to be human beings for each other, seeing the inner reality rather than the outside image.

Another interpretation that was very popular in the thirties, forties, fifties, was that we were the people who could show Western civilization how to live without violence toward each other. Western civilization, at least in this part of the globe, has rather over-glamorized the ideal of the tough (and violent) man, the one who strives with and subdues the land, forcing his way to the top, whatever the cost to others. In a world becoming increasingly aware that this myth has created a desperately sick society, we offer lessons that we learned years ago and that are as natural to gay culture as breathing: men can be tender, nurturing, and sensitive without being weak, and women can be strong, dynamic, and decisive without being violent. I suspect that what people fear the most is the challenge we pose to the traditional gender roles, not our sexuality as such, because rethinking the gender roles might just require people to change and risk acknowledging the parts of themselves they have long rejected.

In a sense, we already have something that we can model. Is this why God created us? No, I don't think so. I think this is a little bonus. Call it a survival adaptation, at which we are superb, by the way. Every openly gay person is a statement about human courage and the human spirit, and what God really has in mind for all human beings. That is what we can model, not the styles of living, dressing, talking, and joking that are so identified with us.

What Color Should a Zebra Be?

When I look again at God's purpose in creating us gay, I first see the profligate creativity of a love so passionate and so intense that it cannot stay inside the lines. Watch very small children with coloring books, and see the sheer delight they have in coloring the zebra purple and the puppy green, slathering on blues and reds and yellows, without worrying too much whether they're staying inside the lines or not. Until, of course, the Elder Siblings sniff and point out that it isn't as neat as their drawings, and anyway, you *can't have* a purple zebra or a lime-green dog. This is, to me, an irresistible image of our queer God's creativity. God takes a great delight in trying something different, in going so far outside the lines that the picture slops over onto the other page. And, of course, the Elder Siblings of the church are sniffing and saying, "You can't have all those messy-looking people here. Dear God, what—what *is* that woman wearing? And—ohmigod! what are those two *doing*?" They have a problem, sure enough, but the problem is not with us, but with God, who didn't consult the Elder Siblings about creation. God can create purple zebras, lavender cowboys, and lipstick lesbians if God has a mind to. And God obviously does.

One of the things that human religion has tended to descend to, over and over, is trying to define exactly where the lines are, and what color the zebras should be, which forces God to keep showing us, over and over again, that there are no lines and that the zebras can even be rainbow-striped. Even we gay and lesbian types have much to learn: I have had to come to terms with the fact that I have been just as ignorant and prejudiced about bisexual and transgendered people as heterosexuals are about me. I suspect we have not even begun to see the full variety even now. The nature of God's creativity is to create wherever there is room to create, and we as gay and lesbian Christians must be just as willing to challenge our lines and our ideas of what color the zebras should be. This is one of the things that become troublesome to gay men and lesbians. I was absolutely clear about the fact, when I came out, that a gay woman had no place in the church if she had the normal number of marbles. God had the last laugh, as usual, and here I am, an Episcopal priest, trying to explain to some of my gay friends why I belong here. As gay men and women, we are unacceptable to much of the church. As Christians, we are unacceptable to much of the gay and lesbian community. We appear to be outside everyone else's lines. It begins to look like a permanent vocation, rather than a mere accident.

Isn't this peculiarly similar to what Jesus warned us about: that we would give scandal to everyone, find no safe place in which to lay our heads, and that it would be the way of greater and greater life? God is a

queer one, a trickster, who always gets the last laugh. We see those poor
benighted fishermen going out to work one day, thinking it is going to
be another routine workday in the old boat, and suddenly finding
themselves yanked into something new. We see Matthew sitting at his
tax-gathering table, adding up numbers, figuring out what his invest-
ments are worth, thinking he can retire to Alexandria, when God yanks
the rug from under him.

At the heart of what we are, whatever that particular thing may be,
we serve a function, especially in the church, in keeping it off-balance,
because we ourselves are kept continually off-balance and have to be
open to what God is going to do next. (Another justification for camp
is that it proves to straight people that being off-balance isn't a tragedy:
it has enormous potential for humor.)

Something to Show the World

Another important reason the church needs gay men and lesbians is
very personal, very immediate, for all of us. This is a world that mili-
tates against wholeness, against any human being becoming who he or
she is. The process of attenuating and crippling people begins in childhood, begins with the denial of our feelings. "Oh, you do not want to
throw your baby sister in the garbage!" Well, you probably did at that
moment. "Now, aren't you sorry you hit Cousin Bobby?" No, not even
remotely. Small children are terribly direct about their feelings, and
sooner or later they are socialized into controlling their feelings, lying
about their feelings, pretending to certain feelings, and then wondering why they live in a state of confusion about what they feel at all.
That's one of the most threatening things about gay men and lesbians,
where straight people are concerned. We're the ones who are supposed
to have given in to our feelings. We horrify mainstream culture with
every fey, playful, imaginative tweak we give the gender roles we wear.
The straight culture desperately needs us to do that for them.

None of us grows up whole. We are educated out of being who we
are, and each of the gay men and women who can stand up and say
who they are is an icon for each of the other human beings who do not
yet have the courage to be who they are, or who have the suspicion that
they are someone other than they have been taught they are. And this
extends far, far beyond sexual identity. It's a very scary thing to challenge the received wisdom of one's entire culture, which is why we are
both the terror and the envy of straight people. In a world in as much
conflict as ours is, one thing that is desperately needed is the visible
presence of people who are not afraid to challenge received wisdom,
which is turning people into economic drones, destroying our envi-

ronment, and pressing the vast majority of human beings to the margins because they have the wrong language, color, or gender.

Until Western religions grant us saints of our own, we must be the saints for one another: the ones who show one another what courage looks like, what integrity looks like, what caring looks like, what nonpossessive love looks like, what it means to be a sexually active, spiritually active Christian. And we offer the same to all those who can see past their own fears and hatreds and are seriously committed to becoming who God intended them to be, conventional or not.

The reason God created gay men and women is simply one more articulation of the whole purpose for which God created *anything*. Every one of us is a living testimony of God's fertile, passionate, and irrepressible love, a living icon of the way that love defines the very essence of who we are and of how love can resist, subvert, and transform the most repressive laws. Do we have questions? Oh, yes! And are there answers? Not the ones you expect.

Why me, God?

Because I love you.

Why did you create me this way?

I just couldn't resist it!

or even that dazzling moment of truth when we finally admit to God:

Guess what, God? I'm gay!

Funny you should mention it. . . .

BILL: EROTIC SPIRIT

Carrying a Culture's Baggage

We who are gay and lesbian are defined by our erotic desires—or at least in *terms* of those desires. There may be many moments in our lives when this seems quite bizarre; there is so much more to life than the erotic. Important as it is, what percentage of our total life span is actually devoted to it, in comparison with, say, the more mundane tasks of washing clothes or carrying out the garbage—or even the other great delights of life such as music and food? Still, the world at large defines us in erotic terms; and that's the area of our own lives where we have at last been able to identify what makes us different from other people.

As a result, we wind up carrying for our culture as a whole the burden of the culture's uncertainties and anxieties about sex. Some of us have the experience occasionally of heterosexual friends assuming that we know everything about sex. Believe me, I don't. I've known a few gay men who may come close to that, but I'm not one of them. But the assumption is that because we've got "sexual" in our cultural title we're the experts. We're homo*sexual*—whereas heterosexual folks tend to think of themselves as just "standard issue," which isn't really the same thing as hetero*sexual*.

Now, there's no reason for gay and lesbian people simply to accept this popular definition of ourselves as the inevitable truth. Whether we think of ourselves as more sexual than other people or not, we shouldn't feel obligated to fulfill all the expectations of the world at large. Still, we cannot deal with who we are in our culture without paying some attention to how we're culturally defined. After all, that's a substantial part of how all human beings are shaped, everywhere, always. Nobody becomes fully human just by virtue of being born with human genes. You have to be brought into the human community. Human beings are always cultural beings. And so if we want to talk about gay and lesbian spirituality, we have to talk about sex, about the erotic. It's too big a piece of who we are to be ignored.

If the truth be told, it's too big a piece of who *all* human beings are to be ignored. Nonetheless, much of Christian spirituality has done its best

74   GIFTED BY OTHERNESS

to set this whole piece aside. I think all sorts of people who are serious about spirituality increasingly understand that you can't do that. For example, people in religious orders speak more and more about their commitment to celibacy not as a negation of the erotic, but as a particular way of living it out. Our age has become aware, thanks to Dr. Freud and others, of how deeply the sexual and erotic elements are rooted in humanity, of how much influence they have, and of what strange shapes that influence can take. There is a broadly based movement, within Christianity and outside it, toward trying to think of sexuality and spirituality seriously in relation to each other; but it's still in its infancy. There isn't any solid conclusion to be drawn at this point. Instead, we who are lesbian or gay have to think of ourselves as pioneers in this area.

One thing that holds us back is our experience of the church as basically negative about sex. What does the church have to say about sex? Well, it says you'd better not do this, and you'd better not do that, and for God's sake, don't do *that*—and don't even *think* about *that*! I once heard the "traditional" Christian sexual ethic (that is, the one most of us heard when we were younger) summed up as: "Sex is dirty, nasty, and disgusting. Save it for someone you love." Actually, the tradition is much older, deeper, and richer than that. But it can be hard to shake off this limited impression we've been given of it. Let me try to help in that process by taking a starting point unfamiliar to most of us.

The Eros of God

I begin, then, with the doctrine of the Trinity. What is the doctrine of the Trinity about? Most of us, if we think of it at all, probably think of it as a form of ecclesiastical higher mathematics. It does funny things with numbers—not necessarily any funnier than, say, calculus—but it's certainly a mystery. It's like what Albert the Alligator in the old Pogo comic strip used to refer to as "trickonometry." But that's really not what it's about. It is a metaphor, to be sure; it is a riddle. All our language about God is a metaphor and a riddle because who knows the detailed truth about God, really? Which of us truly and fully *knows* God? And even if we did, we'd still be left struggling with human language that is ill-adapted to convey anything so surprising and complex. We can't pin God down like a butterfly in a glass case and make detailed measurements and be sure that the same definition is going to apply from one day to the next. I'm told that Islam teaches that there are a hundred names for God, but that one of them has been lost and will never be known. So you can know all the available ninety-nine and still never have it complete.

The Trinity, then, is one way of talking about God. And what is it trying to say? It's not about the mathematical riddle; it's saying that in the

GTU BOOKSTORE
09/26/01   15:19   H   0   12749

RETURNS WITHIN ONE WEEK FOR STORE CREDIT
THANKS AND COME AGAIN!

GTU BOOKSTORE
09/26/01   15:32   H   0   12749
          1@ 16.95 0819218863   10%$ 15.26
                   GIFTED BY OTHERN

SUBTOTAL $ 15.26
SALES TAX @ 8.000% $ 1.22
TOTAL $ 16.48
TENDER Credit $ 14.54
TENDER Cash $ 1.94

RETURNS WITHIN ONE WEEK FOR STORE CREDIT
THANKS AND COME AGAIN!

GTU BOOKSTORE

RETURNS WITHIN ONE WEEK FOR STORE CREDIT
THANKS AND COME AGAIN!

GTU BOOKSTORE
09/26/01   15:32   H   0   12749
1@ 16.95 0819218863   10%*   15.26
          GIFTED BY OTHER*
TENDER Cash   *   1.94

RETURNS WITHIN ONE WEEK FOR STORE CREDIT
THANKS AND COME AGAIN!

beginning, or even before the beginning, God is love. God is a love so powerful, so passionate that it cannot *not* have a beloved. God can't exist without a beloved, and so the Father generates the Son. Or, in language that's better and clearer—language Augustine of Hippo used—the Lover generates the Beloved. And yet the Lover and the Beloved are so perfectly unified that there's still only one God. The power that achieves that is Love itself, which arises in and with the interchange between the Lover and the Beloved. I'd like to see us go back to this language. Not only is it more revealing of the truth, it would also relieve us of the many problems attendant on the language of Father, Son, and Holy Spirit.

The Trinity is the Lover, the Beloved, and the Love that binds all together in One—Love so passionate, so powerful that it cannot be without a beloved. Even within the life of God it cannot be without a beloved. And the love doesn't even stay "inside" the life of God. Even though the life of God is in some sense perfect and complete within God's self, God's love is so passionate, so intense, so perfect, so powerful that it spills over into the creation of the world. The immense variety and beauty and changefulness of the universe is a necessary product of this love. Love wants to enjoy itself in as many ways as possible, to delight in the beloved in as many ways as possible. And something like humanity is necessary, too, because love always longs to be returned. The rocks and the trees return God's love in a certain sense, but there is another sense in which the only beings who can truly return God's passionate love are beings who are free not to return it. And so God takes the incredible risk of creating beings who can say no, who are actually capable of saying no to love.

When we say no to love, it does terrible things to us, because we were, after all, created to love. But we do have the freedom and the ability to say no to love. We have the ability to reduce our lives, to close them in, to cut them off and watch them shrivel up. We *can* do this, but it's not what God created us for. What God created us for is to love God in return and to love one another—indeed to love the whole creation. God is an artist. Can you love the artist and hate the paintings? I don't think it'll work. It means that you haven't figured out who the artist is yet, if you can't see the artist in the paintings. Thomas Traherne in his *Centuries* of meditations says, "God alone cannot be beloved." You can't do it that way. You can't retreat just to the pure, undistracted love of God as if you were God's only creation. To love God means to love the creation, to love one another. Jesus takes these two commandments out of the Torah and puts them together—love God with your whole self, and love your neighbor as yourself.

So this love that spills over in the life of the Trinity and then spills over yet again, out of the life of the Trinity into the creation—this love, for Christians, is the most fundamental thing we can say about God.

There are ways of talking about this besides the doctrine of the Trinity. Indeed, this is the theme that permeates every aspect of the central Christian teachings: the Incarnation, the Atonement, the gifts of the Spirit. But, try as you may, you can't be more orthodox or express the Christian gospel more deeply than by saying "God is love" (1 John 4:8, 16). Any effort to talk about sexuality and spirituality in a Christian context must take this as foundation.

Now you may well have heard it said, at one time or another, that we're not supposed to think that way. "Yes, of course," you were told, "God is love, but not *that* kind of love. God is a very special kind of New Testament love; it even has a special Greek term attached to it. God is *agape* love. And *agape* love is completely different from that other Greek word for love, *eros*." *Eros* is presented, in this context, as something base and grasping. *Eros*, we are told, is love that wants to possess the beloved, whereas *agape* is totally selfless. It wants nothing for itself; it just wants to give. But, for better or worse, that's all bosh. This isn't the way the Greek language worked, despite all of the conventional insistence on it that we've been hearing for about fifty years now.

When you look at the whole of the Greek Scriptures, including the Greek translation of the Old Testament, which is the way most early Christians knew the Scriptures of Israel, you find that the word-group that *agape* belongs to was just the broad language for love in the environment where the New Testament was being written. When the Greek translation of Genesis wants to talk about how Isaac felt about Rebecca when he first saw her, it uses the verb *agapao*. It uses that same verb for how he felt about his sons, too. It's pretty much like the English word *love*—it was a catch-all term.

And all those nasty things that have been said about *eros* as such are not true, either. *Eros* is not simply a grasping kind of love. If you read Greek love poetry, it's like any other love poetry: some of it's grasping, some of it's possessive, and some of it is just dumbstruck with the beauty of the beloved, with intense passion and longing. Yes, of course there is longing. What kind of love is it that doesn't long for the beloved? What kind of love is it that doesn't want to be returned? I'm not sure that would be love at all. In any case, it doesn't fit what we know of God. It may be a sort of Lady Bountiful syndrome projected onto God. (Please excuse the sexism of that particular phrase, but that's the image that's come into our culture. The image of the person who doesn't have enough to do and decides to do good to the poor because the poor can't do anything about it.) And even that condescending kind of love—if it *is* love—wants something of the beloved. It wants the beloved to be dependent. It wants the beloved to be needy, so that I can go on giving and giving and feel terribly good about myself because I'm just like God. I have no limits. I have no limits to my store of love. I'm inexhaustible.

Now, love is love. Greek isn't really any more specific about it than English is. It had more words, but that doesn't mean that they were clearly separated from each other and defined in distinction to one another. Love is love, and sometimes it's erotic in the sense of being sexual, sometimes we think of it as having more to do with friendship, and sometimes it's a more general kind of love that we share with whole groups and with creation at large. But love is love. And love includes admiration. It includes desire, the desire to have our love returned. It wants connection, always. It wants a beloved. It wants to be beloved.

When Love—and Religion—Go Bad

Now, love can go bad, of course. I'm a firm believer in the doctrine of total depravity—which I take to mean not that everything we do is depraved, but that there's nothing human that is immune to being depraved. There's nothing within our human reach that we can't turn somehow to the purposes of sin.

Religion, of course, is one of the foremost examples. It's really easy to turn religion into a sin. We use it all the time to beat up on other people. It becomes an excuse for wars. Even prominent saints have sometimes been implicated in that. We think lovely thoughts of St. Columba going off to his hermitage in Iona. Do you know why he had to go to Iona? He was exiled from Ireland because he had fomented a war between two monasteries over the possession of a book. He had made a copy of a book borrowed from another monastery, and he wanted to keep it. But the judges ruled, in the contemporary legal language, that "the calf goes with the cow." The copy belonged to the monastery that had lent him the original, but Columba refused to give it up and it resulted in a pitched battle. Now, Columba learned from this terrible episode, but the point stands: religion can go bad. For a still worse example, think of Bernard of Clairvaux, who actually preached that Christians ought to go to war in the Crusades and kill people of other faiths. Religion can go bad. And, yes, love can go bad. In Columba's case, it was his love for the book that went bad. At least he accepted his penance and turned it to good.

There's nothing in humanity that can guarantee love against this kind of perversion. Still, love holds more than just our human depravity. Ultimately, love is the power and the goodness that is God's own life. If there's any hope for humanity, it's in this love. It's not inevitable, though. We can say no to love. One way to do that is to say a straightforward no, but our preferred way is to say "Oh, yes, yes, yes" and then twist it around into something else. We can make a terrible mess of love. But love in itself is still the motive power of the universe. There wouldn't even be a universe if it weren't for love. We wouldn't exist except for love. It's the *sine qua non* of everything that is.

This ultimate love is not only powerful and creative; it is passionate. God wants us to return this love. God wants it so badly that God has been willing to become a human being, to be vulnerable to us, to let us do anything we chose to him. And what we chose was to kill God because God's love was too threatening. And yet, even after that rejection, God returns to stay with us and never gives up on us. So there can never be a Christian spirituality that's not erotic, because God has put the *eros* into it from the beginning. If there's no room in it for *eros*, there's no room for God.

If we try to keep our passions out of our relationship with God, perhaps it's because we haven't really been paying attention. We may not really be following Christian teaching so much as we're following Stoic philosophy. There's no denying that Stoicism has continued to have a very strong influence on Christians ever since antiquity. And Stoic philosophy wants us not to have passions. Stoic philosophy wants us to be purely rational, never to be disturbed by anything, not to desire anything very much, to be completely autonomous, completely self-sufficient. That's not the vision of Christian spirituality.

The vision of Christian spirituality is—well, think of the famous sculpture of St. Teresa by Bernini: she's lying back in what certainly appears to be the throes of sexual ecstasy, a cherub standing over her with a dart and looking a whole lot like the classical image of *Eros*. That kind of intense erotic connection, that kind of ecstasy even, is what Christian spirituality is about. It doesn't have to be in Teresa's style, of course. It doesn't have to be so obviously sexual or so intensely sexual. It can present itself in a great many ways. But it's always about love—not some pallid, substitute, empty love, but a love that wants to be connected. God wants to be connected with us; we want to be connected with God. And to love God we have to love God's creation as well. It just doesn't work otherwise.

The Eros of the Bible

To some readers, this may all seem terribly unbiblical. But it's as biblical as it could possibly be. God, in the very beginning, creates human beings as erotic beings. We claim to believe in God the creator: in fact, it's built into the creeds so as to rule out all that gnostic stuff about the creation being evil. But we built the doctrine of creation into the creeds and thought, "Well, that's taken care of," and then went back to being gnostics in practice and thinking of sex as evil. But there it is in the creeds—and in the Bible, too: God is creator. We, as we exist right now, are products of God's creative activity, and the two creation stories at the beginning of Genesis, even though they have different origins and different foci, agree that God made us erotic beings.

Those two creation stories don't agree on much else. The first one, for example, talks about humanity as having been created in the image and likeness of God; the second one talks about humanity as having been created from the dust of the earth and God's breath. The one thing they agree on, the one thing they both emphasize about humanity, is that humanity is sexual. Male and female God made us, according to Genesis 1. And in Genesis 2, God says, "It's not good for the human being to be alone." So God creates the animals, and they're great. Adam names them. Adam likes them. But they're not what Adam really needs. And so God casts Human (that's what the name Adam means) into a stupor, a coma, and removes the second human being from the first human being's side. The two can't help but be drawn together.

So from the very beginning humanity is sexual. You may be thinking, "Yes, but *hetero*sexual." True, that's the picture the authors were working with. But, as we'll see, it makes far less difference to the story than you might suppose.

The first creation story in Genesis 1 has something else to say about human sexuality, and it says it in the form of a commandment to the human beings that they are to be fruitful and multiply and fill the earth and subdue it. This is arguably the only commandment in Scripture that humanity has filled completely—or possibly to excess. Certainly at this point in our history, filling the world is not something we need to try harder on. But the point is that one of the things sex is supposed to be, for humanity at large, is procreative. This is not the same as saying that every sexual act must be procreative. That idea has to seem a little strange in a world as heavily populated as our own, in any case. But this is a command to humanity in general, not to each of us individually. If it were a command to every individual, then we would have to suppose that Jeremiah and Jesus and Paul did wrong in not having children. But the Bible never suggests that.

Eros is indeed procreative, and humanity is indeed procreative. But procreation has to do with a lot more than just conceiving and bearing children. As humans, we are cultural beings, not simply natural beings. No human being is just a product of instincts. Producing a human being takes a lot more than literal physical parents: it takes teachers, physicians, nurses, it takes a world of commerce that can move goods, it takes farmers, singers, artists. It takes a whole lot of people to get any child to maturity in any culture. To be procreative for humanity means not simply bearing children; it means raising up a new generation, and that's a bigger and much more complex thing. It requires a lot more roles than simply father and mother.

A Canadian theologian who died a few years ago, André Guindon, suggested replacing the word *procreative* with the word *generative*. Human *eros*, human sexuality is meant to be generative. It is meant to produce something for human life. If that's what we're asking of it, then it doesn't make too much difference if the part that you produce or I produce is a literal child, or whether it's some other piece of the big cultural puzzle, the big cultural project that it takes to bring infants to maturity.

And don't make the mistake of supposing that the other parts of it are not erotic—they definitely are. I've been teaching for a good many years. Early on I became conscious of something I'd been told beforehand, but hadn't believed: teaching is a very erotic activity. It's one reason, I suppose, that teachers sometimes get in sexual trouble with students, but as Plato observed long ago, the learning process doesn't work nearly as well if there's any actual physical consummation of the *eros*. What you want is to keep the erotic tension; but you are wooing your students when you're a teacher. You're wooing them for a third party, as it were, in the hope that they can catch some glimpse of the beauty and wonder of this topic that you're trying to teach them about. It's an intensely erotic thing.

The erotic is what binds human beings together, quite apart from whether we're remotely interested in a physical consummation of it. The erotic is what binds us together: we desire one another—in a whole lot of different ways. We want our love returned: we want to give it, and we want it returned. Love works only when there's both giving and receiving. If it's content to be totally one-sided, it isn't love anymore. And it not only desires to be returned, it desires to create with the beloved something new that wasn't there before. All love is generative.

The Eros of Friendship

The second creation story in Genesis 2, puts a different spin on the erotic. As we've seen, God is looking here for companionship for the first human being. And the importance of companionship is the same for us all. It will get satisfied for all of us in a great variety of ways. But once again, it's all erotic, regardless of the exact expression it may take. There's another wonderful passage in Scripture about this quality of being human—in Ecclesiastes 4:9–11:

> Two are better than one, because they have a good reward for their toil. For if they fall, one will lift up the other; but woe to one who is alone and falls and does not have another to help.

Again, if two lie together, they keep warm; but how can one keep warm alone? And though one might prevail against another, two will withstand one. A threefold cord is not quickly broken.

Now, what does this mean? That it's bad to be single? No. For a lot of us that's exactly the right state to be in. But it means that even the hermit, in the hermitage, is not truly alone. You carry with you always all the gifts and alas, all the harm, that other people have done you in your life. A hermit who retires to the hermitage at age thirty is going to have a lot of people there with him. In general, for most of us—those of us who do not have that extreme calling to singlehood—life is possible and joyful and delightful because there are other people in it. It's also what makes it aggravating and irksome and tiresome at times; but, as I said before, that's the work of total depravity. Total depravity doesn't wipe out the good; it's just always there alongside it, that's all.

The ability of *eros* to connect people with one another isn't limited by one's sexual orientation. I have a few friends who happen to be heterosexual women; some of them are among my very closest confidantes. I have a few who happen to be homosexual women. I have good friends who are heterosexual men. I have good friends who are homosexual men. And I am an introvert, so we're not talking about six hundred people. An extrovert may have six hundred good friends, but I'm talking about maybe fifteen people. The bonds of friendship, the bonds of work, the bonds of neighborliness, the bonds of citizenship—they don't depend that much on our sexuality. They depend on our ability to be attracted to and to attract other people. The attractions of friendship may be as strong as the attractions of sex, and indeed if a sexual attraction is going to stay strong it usually needs some of the attraction of friendship to go along with it.

So the erotic pervades our human experience, all our relationships with other people. It's also, in particular, the foundation of marriage. I use the word *marriage* broadly here, not referring only to what is legally defined as marriage. For the life of me, when I look at a relative's thirty-five-year partnership or the twenty years together that some friends of mine recently celebrated by exchanging rings, or the ten years that another couple of friends recently celebrated with a union ceremony, I can't see much difference between homosexual partnerships and heterosexual partnerships. They have the same pluses and the same minuses, the same problems, the same joys. They're really not particularly different.

Here's a vivid illustration—a poem by Alice Bloch called "Six Years: For Nancy."

A friend calls us
an old married couple

I flinch
you don't mind
On the way home
you ask why I got upset
We are something
like what she said
you say   I say
No

We aren't married.
No one has blessed
this union   no one
gave us kitchen gadgets
We bought our own blender
We built our common life
in the space between the laws

Six years
What drew us together
a cartographer   a magnetic force
our bodies   our speech
the wind   a hunger

Listeners both
we talked

I wanted: your lean wired energy
control   decisiveness
honesty   your past
as an athlete

You wanted:
my "culture"
gentleness   warmth

Of course that was doomed.
You brought out
my anger   I resist
your control   your energy
exhausts me   my hands
are too hot for you   you gained

the weight I lost   my gentleness
is dishonest   your honesty
is cruel   you hate
my reading   I hate
your motorcycle

Yet something has changed
You have become gentler
I more decisive
We walk easily
around our house
into each other's language
There is nothing
we cannot say together

Solid ground
under our feet
we know this landscape
We have no choice
of destination   only the route
is a mystery   every day
a new map of the same terrain

That account of the dynamics of intimate life-partnership is unusual only in its honesty, its careful observation, and the wonderfully communicative quality of its language. The process of growing together that it conveys is simply human, marked by the uniqueness of the two people, and recognizable without regard to their sexuality.

So Genesis gives us the erotic as generative and the erotic as companionship. But always the erotic is passionate and desiring—desiring the other, desiring connection, desiring the return of our passion. Modern Christians might be willing to rest there, on the assumption that that's the best that we'll get out of Scripture. I suspect that's partly because, like Christians of every age, we tend to be very selective about what we read.

The Song of Songs Which Is Solomon's—and Everybody's

One of the things we don't read very much anymore is the little book in the Scriptures of Israel variously called the Song of Songs or the Song of Solomon. Actually it has both titles within the Hebrew text, "The Song of Songs which is Solomon's." We often think of it as a rather marginal book in the Bible. If you know something about the history of the Bible, you've most likely been told, "Well, it barely made it in. This was one of the last books to be admitted to the Bible, and there was a lot of doubt about it. Probably it was only admitted because it could be treated as an allegory of the love of God for Israel, or the love of Christ for the Church, or the love of God for the individual soul. So don't pay it too much mind."

In the Middle Ages, however, the situation was quite different. The Song of Songs was much read, and a great many commentaries were written on it by both Christians and Jews. This was a time when Christians thought that the Song of Songs, far from being marginal, was one of the central texts in the Bible. And you know, there's no reason it shouldn't be. There aren't any little pointing hands in the margin of the Bible to tell us that, if you want to talk about sex, you must start in this or that particular spot. For some reason, we've got into the habit of starting with the *rules* when we want to talk about the Bible and sex. As we've begun to shed that bad habit, many people have shifted over to Genesis 1 and 2. But there's no reason at all why we can't start with the Song of Songs. And what is the Song of Songs? It may be a great many things. It doesn't have to be just one thing; it's perfectly all right to read it as an allegory. At the surface level, the most obvious level, it's a collection of love poetry. And its language, however ornate and different from ours today, is surprisingly direct.

I often teach an advanced Greek course, using texts from the ancient Greek translation of the Old Testament. One year, we were reading from the Song of Songs. The best student in the course was a young man who had perhaps led a somewhat sheltered life. His command of Greek was excellent, but one day he was upset about his translation. He said, "At least I think that's what it's saying, but it doesn't make any sense." The text runs something like this in translation (the woman's voice is speaking):

> On my bed at night
> I sought the man my soul loved.
> I sought him and did not find him.
> I called him and he didn't respond to me. (3:1)

Then she declares that she will get up, go out, and look for him. I said to him that his translation was perfect—they'd been in bed, she wakes up, he's gone, and she goes out to look for him. He turned quite red and said, "But they're not married yet!" And you know something? He was right. They aren't. The Song of Songs isn't concerned about marriage. It's not worried about fulfilling the rules. It's concerned about the quality of love between the two.

Strangely enough, it's very hard to place the kind of love expressed in the Song of Songs in terms of what we know about the cultural life of ancient Israel. Marriage was about property in that world. A woman passed from the ownership of her father to the ownership of her husband. If a young woman was raped before she was married, that was treated as an offense against her father's property, not as an offense against her. The rapist was required to pay the bride-price to her father, and then if the father chose, he could marry her to the rapist (Deuteronomy 22:28). Obviously, this implies a radically different understanding of sexual ethics from ours. But the Song of Songs is an exchange of love songs between two equals. Oh, the man is referred to occasionally as a prince, or even as a king, but he doesn't act as if this gives him the commanding role. Instead, they have to woo each other. They speak about their longing for each other. There's never any suggestion that one of them is in charge and the other has to go along with it. It's a kind of small miracle in the middle of the Scriptures.

Ever since the Song of Songs was brought into Scripture, Jews and Christians alike have used it over and over and over again as one of the best ways we have of talking about the relationship between us and God. If we want to talk about our intimacy with God and the intensity of that relationship, we typically wind up talking about it in terms of sexual love. For some people that has meant that you treat the love of God as a substitute for sexual love of the ordinary human kind. That's fine if someone actually has that calling and that gift. But if human beings no longer felt sexual passion for one another and if we no longer created sexual love on the basis of that passion, the metaphors of the Song of Songs wouldn't do us any good anymore. Maybe we don't all have to create love through sexual passion, but certainly the human race as such has to. If we quit doing that—if such a dreadful thing should happen to us—we wouldn't know how to talk about our relationship with God anymore. When we take the Song of Songs seriously, we discover that God created human beings sexual so that the delight of our experience with the beloved could give us some hint in our day-to-day experience of what our relationship with God is like.

What a terrible shame that the church has gotten hung up on the rules as if they were the only important things. Now, rules are very useful. I don't mean to dismiss them entirely. As a gay man, I'm probably more suspicious of them than heterosexual people feel a need to be. In my late thirties, I finally recognized that some of the rules I grew up with were in fact wrong. They had been completely misleading, had taken me away from my God-given humanity rather than toward it, had interposed a barrier in my love of God rather than fostering it. Naturally, given that experience, I'm a little skeptical about all of the rules. And yet I think they're useful, because if I'm about to overstep one of them, I have to think very carefully about why I'm doing it. Am I overstepping it because it truly is not helpful? Or am I overstepping it because I'm trying to turn love to my own purposes, turn it from being a genuine gift in search of genuine response into a means of control or self-aggrandizement or any of those other nasty things we make of it?

The rules are useful, but they're not the primary thing. I'm not much of an athlete, but I would imagine that having all the good advice in the world is not in itself going to produce a good golf swing. You have to practice it, and then you make a lot of mistakes, and then somebody helps you with your mistakes—helps you see what you're doing wrong. I imagine this is true, pretty much, with all aspects of athletics. I think probably the same thing is true about love. Should love be the one human thing that we have to get perfectly right the first time? If so, we're in deep trouble. I don't imagine many of us succeed. If it happens, it's pure grace. Most of us are probably going to make a lot of mistakes. Most of us are going to misunderstand what we're doing much of the time. Most of us are going to have to talk with friends and try to figure what's going on in our lives at this particular moment. We are going—with luck, with grace, with the help of God—to mature over the years and come to a clearer understanding of love and a more mature ability to participate in it.

Again, I'm not talking just about sex, but I am talking about sex because it is critical to the whole range of our erotic attractions and relationships. But the rules are not the place to begin. The place to begin is with God, with God's love, which cannot *not* have a beloved, which is incapable of being without a beloved, which is so passionate and so powerful that even the love within the inner life of God, the love within the Trinity, isn't enough. There has to be a creation. Perhaps there have to be many creations. There have to be beings, like us, made in God's image, capable of responding to God's love.

I can't imagine a more compelling statement of our love affair with God than Thomas Traherne's poem "Love." It was written at the end of the seventeenth century, and Traherne does a typical turn of the time and uses classical imagery alongside biblical imagery. He even talks about our relationship to God in terms of Zeus or Jupiter or Jove. Zeus was a great philanderer, and two of his philandering episodes are mentioned in this portion of the poem. One is with Danae, whom he visits as a shower of gold. She becomes pregnant with the hero Perseus. The other is with Ganymede, the beautiful youth who becomes Zeus's cupbearer. Zeus took the form of an eagle and swept him up to the heavens. So we've got one heterosexual and one homosexual image here. It's really quite amazing:

O nectar! O delicious stream!
O ravishing and only pleasure! Where
    Shall such another theme
Inspire my tongue with joys, or please mine ear!
        Abridgement of delights!
            And queen of sights!
O mine of rarities! O kingdom wide!
O more! O cause of all! O glorious bride!
        O God! O bride of God! O king!
        O soul and crown of everything!

        Did my ambition ever dream
Of such a Lord, of such a love! Did I
        Expect so sweet a stream
As this at any time! Could any eye
        Believe it? Why, all power
            Is used here
Joys down from Heaven on my head to shower,
And Jove beyond the fiction doth appear
        Once more in golden rain to come
        To Danae's pleasing, fruitful womb.

        His Ganymede! His life! His joy!
Or He comes down to me, or takes me up
        That I might be His boy,
And fill, and taste, and give, and drink the cup.
        But these (tho great) are all
            Too short and small,
Too weak and feeble pictures to express
The true mysterious depths of blessedness.
        I am His image, and His friend.
        His son, bride, glory, temple, end.

You can't say all that without sexual, erotic language—or without our collective human experience of the reality behind it.

M. R.: TELLING THE STORY, SHAPING THE HISTORY

The Molding of History

One of the things that has fascinated me all of my life, from childhood on, is the way in which story and history are interrelated. I grew up in a family that told stories, especially family stories. I didn't realize how important this was until I began speaking on gay identity, gay spirituality, and gay history. I began to prize the things I took with me out of my childhood.

My basic academic disciplines, before I went to seminary, were literature and history, and I have never been able to choose which holds the greater fascination for me, so I have continued to study—and to teach—both. I find, however, that while most people are willing to live with some decidedly queer and quirky interpretations of literature (since they stay well away from it), they can be horribly shaken by what I have to say about history, even gay history. They accuse me of tampering with facts, because after all, history is the facts. Isn't it?

Well, no, not precisely. First of all, history is an entirely human invention that has no objective existence whatsoever outside the human imagination. We are the only creatures in the entire universe who, to our knowledge, have history. Every other creature has a past, but there's a difference between history and the past. History is the construct that we make by passing these past events through the filter of our imagination and our vision. It is highly selective, highly forgetful, and highly personal.

Think about it: even in the course of twenty-four hours, we don't really remember everything that happened to us during that day. Long intervals are dropped out, certain events are magnified because they are assigned certain meanings. Instead of a strict narrative of the past, such as saying, "Yesterday I opened my eyes, turned over in bed, sniffled, scratched my head and my big toe, closed my eyes again, sighed, got up and . . . " and so on in endless detail of every action of the day, we note only the events we call significant, and say, "Yesterday I started a new job." Out of thousands of events, we select just those that seem significant or those that seem to fit the pattern we expect to see. That's exactly the way human history works. A vision, a lens, a grid, is superimposed on life for us, and this lens allows us to select, out of all those millions of single chaotic events, just the ones that seem to have pattern and meaning to us.

What this means is that history is not fixed, but remarkably malleable. (And this is where people start getting upset.) I can only suggest that you read an American history book that was written a hundred years ago, and you'll see how events and their significance have changed. Likewise, if you could see a history book a hundred years from now, you would discover that what we are living through is very different from what you thought. Studying history in the ordinary way creates the illusion that people were much more in the know about things and that it was always clear to them what was going on. The neat textbook divisions are misleading. Because we turn over the last page of chapter 6 and say, "Oh, thank God! We finally finished with the Middle Ages. I can hardly wait to start the Renaissance," we have the illusion that the people who were alive then were equally glad to get out of the Middle Ages and into the Renaissance. But of course, they hadn't the vaguest idea that they were living in the Middle Ages and wouldn't have known the Renaissance if they tripped and fell face-down in it. People in the Scriptures are the same way: they didn't know they were living in Old Testament times. Like you and me, they simply thought they were living in the present, and they looked at the world through that lens.

History, Story, and Identity

There is a second important thing to understand about history: it is one of the things that helps confer and shape our very identity. Quite simply, it's shared history that helps a group of people know who they are, develop a common sense of past and future, and define the very shape of their community.

No people can exist without a history. History is an irreducible part of what actually forms a *group* into a *people*. You simply can't have an identity as a people without a history. This is very evident in the Old Testament world, as we read those stories that seem to be a wonderful, flowing stream of events. Scholars now tell us that they were in fact carefully stitched together from numerous separate tribal traditions and stories. The stitching together had to be done in order to form a larger group identity: the people of the Abraham stories joining their past and future to the people of the Joseph stories, the people who came out of Egypt joining their stories to those who had remained in Canaan. The people who told those stories were probably, at one point, quite separate. In order to claim an identity as "the people of Israel," they had to create a history that would encompass all of them. So the multicolored strands were drawn together and woven into a new fabric. At the same time, a number of strands were simply dropped. The Hagar narrative, for instance, comes to an abrupt and surprising end. It represents a tradition that no longer forms a part of the Israelite identity. Yet Hagar's story is preserved and elaborated in the Hadiths of Islam, as part of what defines Muslim identity.

The Power to Create a People

The whole point is, if you cannot create history, you cannot create a people. We tend to forget that, because most of us acquire our identity quite unconsciously and automatically, especially through the official history we learn in school. This is exactly why history began to fascinate me.

I am a first generation Hungarian-American. My parents were born in Hungary, my grandparents, my great-grandparents, and on back to the invasion of those tough little Mongol horsemen who swept in from the fringes of Asia in the tenth century. At a certain point, it began to occur to me that the history I learned in school, which I firmly accepted as *my* history, had to do with the Pilgrim settlers and the Sons of Liberty and the Abolitionists, which had nothing to do with my biological history at all. It was not my parents' history or my grandparents': 1620 and 1776 had nothing whatever to do with my ancestors, since they didn't arrive here until this century.

I danced between my true-blue American history and the darker, more tragic history of the Magyar people who were slaughtered at Mohács and died in Hitler's slave labor camps. I was told stories of the Reformers, who risked everything for religious principles, and the loyal Catholics who resisted the Reformation at the cost of their lives. Then I became a member of the Fayyad'din order and rooted myself in a history that began in Turkey in 1248, and still later, a Quaker, whose history began in Lancashire, England, in 1652. In becoming an Anglican, I have had to assume a different history. And that is precisely how history works. Without being able to assume a community's history, we cannot really have a sense of being part of that community.

This is one of the ways in which Scripture has more than simply a religious function: it was this set of images and stories that gave people a sense of past and a conviction about the purpose and destiny of their lives.

The church itself began as a group without a coherent history because it consisted of people with widely different histories: Jews from Jerusalem and Greeks from Asia Minor, Romans from Ostia and Egyptians from Alexandria, as well as displaced people who had no

clear idea at all of what their background was. The telling of the stories
and the preservation of the past were enormously important not simply
to preserve the teachings of Jesus, but also to build a strongly knit sense
of identity that could encompass all the disparate elements.

A People Shorn of History

Understanding these aspects of history becomes particularly important
when you begin to consider that we as gay men and lesbians have been
shorn of our history (or perhaps have simply been sliced out of other
people's histories). There is not a single openly identified gay man or
lesbian in either the Old or New Testaments, so thoroughly has our
presence been blotted out of existence, a powerful way of denying our
right to exist at all.

It has been, therefore, exceedingly difficult for gay and lesbian
Christians to convince the church that we are an actual and distinct
minority, a people. We are not defective heteros. We are perfectly normal gay and lesbian people. So the question becomes, how do we arrive
at a history, a narrative, that includes us? We can't just make one up out
of thin air, any more than the Israelites who fled from Egypt could.

Scripture has always been a resource for people in search of an identity, in search of a history, in search of a God. The closest parallel I can
think of is what happened in the United States with the slaves who were
brought over from Africa. They were people who had been uprooted
from their own histories, their own families, their own tribes. It is in
itself a powerful statement that white Americans refer to these people
as a monochromatic group, "the slaves," as if they were an indistin-
guishable mass. They emphatically did not see themselves that way in
the beginning. They were people deeply embedded in different traditions and languages, proud of tribal achievements, rooted in the past
of their own people. The first act of deliberate genocide rested on the
suppression of their language and religion, the separation of members
of tribal groups so that their histories would effectively be lost within
a generation, thereby rendering them even more powerless and docile.

Fortunately, the slave owners assumed that introducing their slaves
to Christianity would make them more docile yet, especially when they
could quote, "Slaves, obey your masters," and, "If someone strikes you
on one cheek, offer him the other." Oh, yes, this would make them meek
and biddable. The great irony was that they had placed in the slaves'
hands the most radical, dangerous, and subversive document on earth!

In the African slaves' story, we see a clear illustration of the gospel of
subversion. Because what happened to them is exactly what happened to
the fugitive slaves from Egypt and the ragtag of the Gentile Mediterranean.

These enslaved, uprooted people, with no history of their own, had been handed an incredibly incendiary resource in the Old Testament. They appropriated the text and made its history theirs. Think, for a moment, of the power of some of the spirituals they wrote and sang in plain sight and hearing of their masters: "Go down, Moses . . . ," "Let my people go . . . ," "There is a balm in Gilead . . . ," "There's a great jubilee a-comin.'" Think of the slave-owning family smiling patronizingly while their slaves danced and sang, "O Mary, don't you weep, don't you mourn. Pharaoh's army got drownded!" Amen!

At the core, they were able to appropriate images that were no more theirs historically than American history is mine biologically. History happens in the creative leap of the imagination. The appropriation of that biblical text by the African American community sustained and gave it a future in which it believed fiercely. It seized the images of the enslaved Israelites, for whom God has the powerful deliverer. It wielded the words of the prophets like weapons. Can anyone hear the recording of Martin Luther King Jr., quoting the prophet Amos and not be moved: "Let justice roll down like a river, and righteousness like an ever-flowing stream"? It brings the hair up on the back of your neck, because that text is so deeply embedded in our culture, is so powerful, that it becomes the basis of a people's history, and its power is ours to appropriate.

What you and I and other gay and lesbian Christians are about is something very similar. We who have been shorn of our history must create one. Not out of thin air, but out of the word, the presence, the reality of God, and God's astonishing and passionate love for those who have been forced to the margins. We can claim the history of deliverance because we represent exactly those people whom God has always called out to. Those who were no people become God's people, like the children of Israel. They were not just people from the Jewish tribes, but the rag-tag, the people of uncertain origins, the ones who had fallen to the bottom of society. The same is true of the believers in the early church. Many of them had been disenfranchised in their own world. You see this over and over again as Paul reminds them that the ones who were called were not the ones at the top of the heap, the wise, the educated, but the poor and the humble. And out of those leavings, God creates a people.

What God Is Up To in the Gay Community

I am convinced that this is exactly what is going on in the gay and lesbian community in the church. The people of God are continually reshaped as God calls and creates a new people in its midst. The Israelites who had remained across the Jordan were not thrilled with those returning weirdos out of Egypt with their strange new ideas. After all, they were people who didn't even know who their parents or their grandparents were. The Jewish Christian community was aghast at the thought of sharing fellowship with uncircumcised Gentiles, just as many white Christians are horrified at the thought of sharing their churches with Christians of color. Is it so surprising that straight Christians, who have had it all their own way for a number of centuries, are so agitated about the thought that they may actually have to accept gay and lesbian Christians in their midst? And is it not fairly obvious that however long or fiercely people resist allowing the new people in, sooner or later God's call will have its way?

Part of becoming God's gay people, of creating a strong and healthy gay Christian identity, begins with the moment at which we stop letting other voices use Scripture to tell us who we are, and go to Scripture ourselves, to let it tell us—and them—who we are.

A friend of mine once said something that I absolutely adore! "No English-speaking Christian ever took up a Bible except to bash another Christian on the head with it." As a gay woman I've had my share of being bashed by Scripture. It's important for us to understand that no one owns Scripture, that every single one of us has the right to appropriate it. The Christians had no qualms whatever about appropriating the texts of the Hebrew Scriptures; they did it so successfully that most Christians do not even view this as a high-handed bit of thievery.

This act of appropriation involves individuals as well as communities. You often see this when you're teaching. There are some people who take reams of notes about the Scripture, demand all the historical references, and never quite get the point of what it's about. Then there are the students who seize the document (or let it seize them), and you can watch the fireworks go off. We never possess understanding. Sometimes we let it possess us.

So what this lesson is about, really, is trying to let a new understanding of Scripture possess us, suggesting a few modest samples of how one gay woman can take a piece of Scripture you've probably heard for years, appropriate it to make it a new vessel for self-understanding, and give us a strong hint of what God may be calling us to be.

The Child Who Passed for an Egyptian

Although I could have started at many places, the story that I've arbitrarily chosen is that of Moses, a child who was never supposed to live in the first place. Think about that for a moment. The intention of the people in power was that Moses would simply cease to exist. You remember the story: Pharaoh sends out the decree that all baby boys in the Israelite community are to be killed. I wasn't exactly a baby boy; nevertheless, a gay child wasn't what anybody in my family planned on. They expected someone else, a generic little heterosexual. I often think of what a day it will be when someone asks the new parents, "What is it?" and instead of just saying, "It's a boy," or "It's a girl," they'll say proudly, "It's a little dykelet," or "It's a baby queen."

What actually happens in the story? We tend to get a bit hung up on the baby sent out on the water in his little ark of bulrushes and miss the startling part: he is rescued by the enemy, Pharaoh's own daughter, a member of the royal house that has decreed Moses' death. She picks up the baby, falls rapturously in love with him, adopts him, and raises him as an Egyptian. Moses passes for Egyptian all the way into adulthood. Does this begin to sound familiar? Moses survives by not looking and acting like what he is, but by looking, talking, and acting as Egyptian as he can. Was Moses aware of his real identity? The story doesn't tell us, but it does tell us that his sister Miriam kept contact with him and that his own mother was probably his wet nurse.

Moses does quite well as long as he stays within the bounds of being Egyptian, and if he can just keep up the pose, all might remain well. But Moses' people are suffering, and God has heard that suffering. And one day, Moses comes across a man he thinks is one of his own people—an Egyptian—beating one of his *real* people, and something inside him snaps.

If you have never read Christopher Fry's play *The Firstborn*, I urge you to.[3] It's a marvelous piece of theater, not the usual story of the Exodus at all, but the story of Moses' return and reunion with his foster family: his foster-mother, the late Pharaoh's daughter, the present Pharaoh, who was the brother of his childhood, and Pharaoh's first-born, the little boy he had loved like his own son. In telling the story of what happened to him, Anath-Bithiah, Moses' Egyptian mother, recounts how, when he looked into the face of the slave who was being beaten, an inner knife scoured his eyes clean, and he saw that the face above his cradle was not her face at all, and that voices descending on him were the voices of ancestral Abraham. Convulsed by the revelation, Moses kills his Egyptian self in the person of the overseer, and tries to conceal him in the sand.

For many of us that is a very apt description of what happens at the moment when we are finally faced with who we are. We realize that we are not the person we have spent a lifetime pretending to be. The voice, the face above the cradle, and the God who descends on us are not those of Egypt. As Moses buries the evidence of his crime, we too may attempt to conceal the truth of what we have learned. But when it finally becomes impossible to conceal it any longer, we, like Moses, are forced to flee into the wilderness.

Exiles and fugitives though we are, we learn to survive in the wilderness. Moses finds a family, marries into it, and to all intents and purposes becomes a Midianite shepherd. He is safe from Egypt—or so he thinks. But though Moses can flee Egypt, he cannot flee God, and the tireless hunter finds him even in the wilderness. God not only speaks to him, but reveals a new name: not the gods of Egypt, not even a god whose name he has ever heard. This God speaks to him out of a bush that is on fire but does not burn, and calls him. Moses approaches cautiously, and this voice says, "I have heard the cries of my people." The voice tells Moses he must return to Egypt, to bring God's people out.

This is not great good news to Moses. It is downright terrifying. But God persists: it is you, precisely you, who must go back and bring my people out.

And so the reluctant prophet returns, to deliver a people he barely knows from—what else?—the power of his own family. (Or rather, his foster family, the people who loved and raised him.) Pharaoh the enemy is in fact the foster-brother of his youth, and the firstborn—the child who must die—is the nephew he loves. Remember this: it is our story, not the version that skips over this detail, and which is told by the heterosexual church. *Delivering his people is almost too costly for Moses to bear.* In a harrowing last scene in *The Firstborn,* Moses desperately tries to save the nephew he loves, only to watch, powerless, as the death of the firstborn crumples the boy at his feet. In an agony of recognition, he cries, "I followed a light into blindness."[4] Freedom is not cheap for Moses. It is not easy, and it is not accomplished in the company of strangers. Freedom happens when we finally face those of our own families, households, churches, congregations, the people we most love, and demand our freedom to go and worship God and become the people God intended.

In the Exodus story, the constant tug-of-war between Moses and Pharaoh builds an incredible tension at the heart of the narrative, until finally, with the death of the firstborn, Pharaoh agrees to release the children of Israel. They go free, but Pharaoh immediately changes his mind and pursues them, and there is the last great scene at the shore of the Sea of Reeds, when the waters part and the children of Israel go free, while the children of Egypt die in the returning waters.

No Christian can overlook that tragic death, by the way, because God created the Egyptians out of the selfsame love that created the Israelites, and the death of the Egyptians was as much a grief to God as to the Egyptians themselves. Freedom is costly, to the straight community as well as to the gay community. It is painful to confront who we are and discover we are not who we thought we were. It is just as painful for those of our own households or faith to realize that we are not what they thought we were, either.

The act of taking these stories as our stories and our right will cause a great deal of pain, but in the end even the church itself does not have the right to tell our story. It is ours to do, for God has given us that right.

That's just one way in which this text, which has been used to bang so many people over the head, becomes a door opening into a deeper understanding of God's compassion and our call to be our own deliverers. Like Moses, we are not asked to confront our enemies, but those of our own household of faith, who may or may not hear God's voice saying, "Let my people go."

A Word of Reassurance

Hear God's words to a people who have been deprived of spiritual life, and who have been dead for a long, long time:

> The hand of the Lord came upon me, and he carried me out by his spirit and put me down in a plain full of bones. He made me go to and fro across them until I had been round them all; they covered the plain, countless numbers of them, and they were very dry. Then the Lord said to me, "Mortal, can these bones live?" And I answered, "Only you know, Lord God." And the Lord said to me, "Prophesy to these bones. Say to them: O dry bones, hear the word of the Lord. This is the word of the Lord God to these bones:
>
> I will put breath in you, and you shall live. I will fasten sinews on you, I will bring flesh upon you, and overlay you with skin, and put breath in you, and you shall live; and you shall know that I am the Lord."
>
> So I began to prophesy as he had bidden me; and as I prophesied, there was a rustling sound, and the bones fitted themselves together, and as I looked, sinews appeared upon them, and flesh covered them, they were overlaid with skin. But there was no breath in them. Then God said to me, "Prophesy to the wind, prophesy, mortal, and say to the wind:
>
> "These are the words of the Lord God: Come, O wind, come from every quarter, and breathe on these slain, that they may come to life." And I began to prophesy as he had bidden me, and breath came into them, and they came to life, and they rose to their feet, a mighty host.
>
> And the Lord said to me, "Mortal one, these bones are the whole people of Israel. They say, 'Our bones are dry, our thread of life is snapped, our web is severed from the loom.' Prophesy,

therefore; say to them, These are the words of the Lord God: O my people, I will open your graves, and I will bring you up from them; and I will restore you to the land of Israel. And you will know that I am the Lord, when I open your graves, and bring you up from them, O my people. And I will put my spirit into you, and you shall live. I, the Lord, have spoken and I will act." *(Ezekiel 37:1–14)*[5]

The word of the Lord.

Thanks be to God!

BILL: READING WITH NEW EYES

The Unpredictable Word

The point that M. R. has made about history as interpretation, history as the way in which we reconceive the past in order to create a present, applies also to our reading of documents from the past, particularly to our reading of Scripture. It's funny how what's on the page in Scripture isn't always the same from one reading to the next. It can change from one moment in your life to another. Anyone who is my age, who has been reading Scripture for years, has probably had this happen more than once. You suddenly see things on the page you never noticed before. You'd have sworn they weren't there last week. But you've had that same Bible for twenty years, so they must have been!

St. Augustine spoke of Scripture as having about it a quality of incredible, amazing depth, shallow enough for lambs to wade in, deep enough for elephants to bathe in. There is no point at which you get to the bottom of Scripture, no point at which you get to the end of it. Always it has something more to tell you. A big reason for that, of course, is that our lives change. As our lives change, our perspectives change, and we see things that we couldn't see from the spot where we were standing even a week ago.

Nobody ever just reads what's on the page. If we're reading carefully, we're making an approximation of it, and we're trying to get closer and closer to it. But careful reading is always a bit like a conversation. A good conversation can take a fair amount of work, because the person you're talking with is not seeing the world exactly the same way you are. Sometimes they're not even using the language the same way that you are. I had a conversation a few years back with another gay man, where we seemed to be saying exactly opposite things about gay male partnerships, and I couldn't figure out why we were at such opposite ends of the spectrum. Finally one of us figured out that I was using the word *relationship* to cover a broad spectrum—everything from one-night stands to lifelong monogamy—and the word *partnership* for consciously undertaken commitments of fidelity, and he was using those two terms in exactly the opposite way. Sometimes it's as simple as that, but not often! To some degree, each of us is living in a world that looks a little different from everyone else's, because we're all standing in slightly different places. And the Bible looks a little different depending on where you're standing.

This may seem very strange. It's probably not what you were taught to expect. For some centuries now, Christians have tried to read Scripture as if it had only one meaning. That habit got started in the late Middle Ages. Before that, people were quite happy for it to have hundreds of different meanings. But in the late Middle Ages and the Reformation, people began to want Scripture to serve a new purpose—the purpose of settling theological disputes. So increasingly, we wanted Scripture to have one meaning to each passage. For quite some time, the church was the authority on all that, and the church would tell you what the one meaning was. It probably had something to do with doctrine, maybe something to do with morals; but there was one meaning for the passage. Later on, academics took charge, and the Scripture still had one meaning, but it was less likely to have to do with doctrine and morals and more likely to have to do with the life and history of a particular ancient community. Either way, the assumption was, "There is one meaning."

And you could hang onto that, at least in the old days in Europe where everybody in this principality was Reformed and everyone in that principality was Lutheran, and everybody in this kingdom was Anglican and everybody in that kingdom was Presbyterian. So in any given part of Europe there was something to hang onto in that way: there was one church to tell you what was right. Later on, the academics all disagreed with each other (it's part of our job description) but basically we approached matters in very similar ways. We might argue about details, but we assumed there was one right reading of the passage and that we could argue each other into acknowledging it if we just kept at it long enough.

But if we expect from the Scriptures what Christians expected of it for the first thousand or more years of our history—not a final answer to a doctrinal question, but some surprising word of grace—then we should expect that there is more to it than one meaning per passage. We should expect to be surprised, even perhaps disoriented at times by our reading of Scripture. We should expect the text on the page to become new as our own experience, and with it our powers of insight, change. The Spirit leads us, in part, through our own life-experience. If we can acknowledge that, we will not only recover and create our own history as gay and lesbian people; we will also bring the whole church something of value out of our own experience.

Jesus and the Person Blind from Birth

Let me take, as example, a familiar story from the ninth chapter of the
Gospel of John, the story of a man who was born blind. As Jesus and
his disciples arrive in Jerusalem, they happen to see a beggar who has
been blind from birth. The disciples have a question: "Whose sin caused
this man to be born blind? Was it his sin, or was it his parents' sin?"
Jesus says to them, "Neither this man nor his parents sinned. He was
born blind that God's works might be revealed in him." And he goes to
the man and spits on the ground and makes a little mud with the saliva,
spreads it on his eyes, and tells him, "Go wash in the Pool of Siloam."
And the man does it! He has to find his way across town to the pool of
Siloam, but he's sufficiently engaged with what Jesus has just done to
him that he goes. When he has washed, he receives his sight. And when
he returns, he immediately becomes a big problem, because the whole
story has taken place on the Sabbath.

The religious authorities can spot potentially disruptive events from
miles away, of course. They want to know what's going on, so they
cross-examine the man about what happened. He tells them, and some
of the authorities say, "This Jesus-person is not from God! Why, he
doesn't observe the Sabbath." (That's one of the ten commandments,
after all. We Christians have gotten so used to ignoring it that we forget that fact, but in the world of Jesus it was a serious offense to violate
the Sabbath.) Others say, "Well, but how can a man who is such a sinner perform such a miracle?" So even among the authorities there is
conflict. They call the man's parents to make sure he was really born
blind, and they cautiously respond, "Yes, he was blind, but don't ask us
what's happened to him. We don't know anything about that."

So they again call the man who'd been born blind and say, "Give glory
to God! We know this man is a sinner." They're really putting the pressure on, and the blind man cooperates as much as he can without denying what had happened to him. He answers, "I don't know whether he's a
sinner. One thing I do know—I used to be blind, and now I can see."
There's a further cross-examination, and finally they say to him, "You
were born entirely in sin, and are you trying to teach us?" and they drive
him off. Jesus hears that he's been thrown out, goes to find him, and says,
"Do you believe in the Son of Man?" (This is very typical of the Gospel
of John—an apparent non sequitur!) It doesn't sound as if the blind man
has ever *heard* of the Son of Man, but his response is, "And who is he, sir,
that I may believe in him?" Jesus says, "You have seen him, and the one
speaking with you is he." He says, "Lord, I believe," and he worships.

The story ends, oddly enough, by going back to the religious authorities. Jesus says, "I came into this world for judgment, so that those who

do not see may see, and those who do see may become blind." Some of
the religious authorities are close enough to overhear him; and they say
to him—one imagines a somewhat huffy tone of voice—"Surely we're
not blind, are we?" Jesus says to them, "If you were blind, you would
have no sin. But now that you say, 'We see,' your sin remains."

Opening the Eyes of the Blind

There was a time when people read this story as one more proof of the
divinity of Jesus. The Gospel of John contains a whole series of *signs*—
miracles meant to validate the claim, early in the gospel, that Jesus is
the incarnate Word of God. There was a time when that would probably have been enough to glean from the passage—one more reinforce-
ment of a basic Johannine doctrine. Perhaps if you are one of those
folks who really like drawing lines in the sand, you might have taken it
a step further and said that it proves that Judaism is all wrong. In that
case, you'd be assuming that it was all about Christian doctrine. Later
on, academic writers about the Gospel of John used this passage primarily to show that the Gospel of John was written in a Jewish-
Christian community that was in the process of being expelled from
the larger Jewish community. The man born blind is the first follower
of Jesus to suffer this fate by being expelled from the community of
study and worship in the synagogue. Earlier in the story, we are told that
his parents' lack of courage arose from the fact that they had heard that
anyone who confessed Jesus would be thrown out of the synagogue.

Any or all of these statements about the meaning of the passage may
make sense to certain people in certain times and places. But if that's
all that John is trying to do here, there certainly is a lot of wasted verbiage. I didn't become aware of how important and how revelatory
some of this apparently wasted verbiage is until my own coming out.
Coming out is a very odd experience—and hard to explain to anyone
who hasn't gone through it. It's difficult and yet it brings with it great
blessings. Coming out means that gay men and lesbians have to come
into touch with something inside themselves that is so true and so profoundly important that, even if we've been avoiding it for decades and
even if our culture tells us this cannot be true (or that, if it is true, it's a
very bad thing), despite it all, we find ourselves having to say, "No, this
is true about me. And it's not wrong or evil or even, in the deepest
sense, a problem." We may say this with great fear and trembling at the
beginning. But the extraordinary thing is that the recognition of all this
turns out to be a blessing. We discover a new kind of grounding and
centering in ourselves. We discover a new coherence in ourselves. Many
of us find ourselves newly or more profoundly connected with God. We

know this is not according to traditional Christian doctrine and traditional ideas of Christian moral practice, and yet it's so true, so profound, it reaches so much into the depths of our souls and spirits, that to deny it would be to deny God.

Having had that experience—indeed, still living in that experience, for it doesn't happen once and then go away—I have found myself reading this gospel story again, and the details suddenly became very important. There are plenty of miracle stories in which Jesus just heals somebody. A little earlier in John's Gospel Jesus heals a man who's been paralyzed for eighteen years, and he doesn't demand much of him. He heals him and tells him to get up and pick up his cot and carry it with him. In other stories of healing in the Gospels, Jesus asks nothing at all. In this story, he demands of this man born blind a very difficult kind of participation in his own healing. He is still blind, his face is covered with mud, and he has to find his way across town to the Pool of Siloam (a name that John tells us means "sent"!) and wash. And then when he comes back, he finds himself in the middle of this terrible hubbub.

Challenging Authority

Jesus clearly offered a major challenge to the leaders of established religion; the blind man's healing concretizes that challenge. He *is* that challenge, all wrapped up in one human being. So the authorities try very hard to bring him back into line. The disciples wanted to do something like that in the beginning, themselves. They're really no better. They want Jesus to settle whether it was the man's parents who had sinned, or whether he was personally responsible for his misfortune. They want to get this thing figured out so that they can put this man into the right pigeonhole and keep their theology tidy. The authorities want to get it figured out so that they can put *Jesus* into the right pigeonhole. Then they'll feel they know exactly who and what he is. Is Jesus a sinner because he ignores the Sabbath, or is he a saint because he healed the man? They try to get the man to help them put Jesus in the right pigeonhole. But finally the man says, "I don't know whether he's a sinner. One thing I do know: I used to be blind, and now I can see."

Here is a beggar, without education, without any social status or political clout. And he's willing to go toe to toe with the established religious leaders because he's received a gift from God so profound, so transformative, that he can't go back on it. If he is forced to choose between religion as it's been taught and this moment of experiencing God's grace, he will choose the experience of God's grace. Does he know who Jesus is? No, not really. Does he have Jesus to run to for protection? No. Jesus is under as much threat as he is. He's out there by himself.

Even his parents have completely lost their courage. You'd think they'd at least be pleased that their son could get a regular job now, but they won't take up for him at all. Still, he says, "God has done this for me, and I will not back down on it. One thing I know: that I was blind and now I see." And hanging onto that one thing was enough for him to stand up to the world.

So when Jesus does find him again and says, "Do you believe in the Son of Man?" he answers, "Who is he, so that I may believe in him?" He can't trust the church anymore, but he trusts Jesus, he trusts the experience of grace. Incidentally, he doesn't leave the church—it throws him out, if you notice that element of the story. He's not interested in abandoning the established religion; the established religion abandons him.

And now that little, concluding exchange with the religious leadership begins to mean a whole lot. In those few words, Jesus addresses the worst temptations of established religion. He's not talking about Judaism as distinct from Christianity here; Christianity is just as prone to this sin as Judaism is. He's talking, rather, about the tendency of religion as such to put itself in charge and exclude grace. This is *our* tendency as church. It's not just some bad hierarchs who do this; it's *we* as church who do this. We think we know about God, we think we've got God all sewed up, we think we've got it settled. The only remaining question is how to get everybody in the right pigeonhole.

No. Jesus said to them (to us, too), "If you were blind, you would have no sin. But now that you say, 'We see,' your sin remains."

Living as One Who Begins to See

This is not an easy teaching for the church. But it has great spiritual value, both for the church and for gay men and women. It reminds us that God is always free, that God is always love, that God is always gift, that God is always surprise. It doesn't mean religion is a bad thing. Religion has preserved the Gospel of John for us to read—and so to rediscover that religion is not enough. Religion is not necessarily a bad thing. But it's not God. The Bible is not God. The church is not God. None of our systems is God. God remains eternally free to give whatever gifts God wishes at whatever moment to whatever person. If religion is doing its job, it will help us to notice when that's happening. If religion is doing its work, it will help us honor the gift in the people whom the grace of God has touched.

So the details of John's story become truly revelatory for me. The blind man isn't offered an easy out. He has to be involved in his own healing. He has to take risks, without knowing how they'll turn out. And then, having done that, he finds that his problems are far from

over. He's become offensive to the religious leadership because he represents their own uncertainty about how to deal with these religious
"irregularities" that Jesus keeps committing. And yet, he knows that he
really has no choice. If he denies this amazing thing that's happened to
him, he will also lose the new life it has granted him. He'll live the rest
of his years as a lie. It's too bad that the religious leadership can't live
up to the high standard the ignorant beggar has just set, but that's their
business, not his.

I come away from this text thinking that the presence of gay and lesbian people in the church is not so very different. We have to participate in our own healing by taking the risk of coming out, insofar as that
is possible for us, of living as the people God has made us. We come
under great pressure to deny what God has done for us. Sometimes the
penalties can be quite grave. But in the long run, we represent, in our
time and place, the necessary grasp, however feeble and uncertain, on
the truth of God's grace. Our experience gives the church a chance to
rejoice with us—and so to reclaim the humility and delight that go with
acceptance of God's grace. We are a challenge to the church at large to
give up playing God and reclaim the ability to see what's going on
under its own nose. The grace God has shown us turns out to be a gift
meant for the church as well.

M. R.: GOD'S GAY TRIBE

Crossing the Sands: Another Sufi Parable

This is the lesson on crossing the sands. Remember it.

The sands are wide, the oases few. It is always safest to remain where you are.

But if you cannot remain where you are, then it is safest to go with a caravan. But if there is no caravan, then it is safest to go with a band of trusted companions. But if there are no trusted companions, then it is safest to go with one who knows the sands. But if there is no one who knows the sands, then you must cross the sands alone.

There are two things to remember. First, take nothing with you but what sustains you: food and water. If you cannot take both, leave the food but carry the water. You must carry the water if you are to cross the sands. Second, never attempt to travel by daylight: the sun will kill you. You must wait until nightfall; then it will be safe to travel. Moonlight and darkness will be light enough.

There are two things you must do. Stay alive. And keep moving. If you can do just those two things, you will come to another oasis.

This is the lesson on crossing the sands. Remember it.

This is an old lesson; I would have known that even if no one had told me so. It has that feel of old things, like some primitive and age-worn talisman rubbed smooth by centuries of handling, all its details worn away by countless hands, until only the essential shape remains. I have never even tried to guess how many travelers before me have survived the journey with no more than this. I pray (because no journey should begin without a prayer) that others will pick up this token, and that its lesson will preserve them through the journey. The sands are wide: without one another's wisdom we would perish there.

I begin here, as the only honest place to start, for any other starting place would be a kind of spiritual evasion. This is not, at core, an exercise: it is a faithful attempt to enter the sands and mark a pathway that, God willing, will in time provide a safer passage for some other soul. To have learned a lesson is to be accountable for handing it on to another. If I learned nothing else from the traveler who taught it to me, I have learned this much.

I am a gay woman who has made that perilous and lonely journey through the sands more than once. I have a spiritual obligation now to tell the story. We, more than most people, have a desperate need to pass this kind of wisdom on; too much of it has been deliberately buried, too much lost in the silence of our lives. We are a people whose entire past has been eradicated. We must dig deep, unearth it, fit the broken fragments back together as best we can, preserve it, pass it on, so that never again will one of ours be left to perish in the desert for the lack of vision.

I have come to understand this as the first task in the shaping of gay ministry. Other ministries—the pastoral, political, social, and sacramental—have important places for us. But the fact is, we as a people have been cheated of our spiritual core, our deep communal memory of knowing we are God's gay tribe. This is, for us, the place where wholeness has to start.

It must, moreover, start with what we have, not wistful glances at the things that we have lost and may never quite recover. Hence, this contradictory beginning: that a Christian woman, born gay by God's grace, should have to start with teaching parables she learned from a Muslim man, as gay as she, who drew them from the Sufi disciplines. It is a desert way, that is the essential thing, a way peculiarly suited to chartless journeys, where the maps do not yet exist. In Christian terms, we travel in the best of company here, as followers of one who did not run from the confrontation in the wilderness, nor draw back when his calling to obey the will of God led him to step outside the boundaries of his own traditions.

John Boswell, in another work that draws the first lines of a map on unmapped territory, likens us to that other group whose experience in Christian culture has been marked by alternate acceptance and persecution: the Jews.[6] Their fortunes have, in many ways, run parallel to ours in Western European culture, sometimes left in peace and sometimes singled out to be the focal point on which irrational fears and hatreds can be vented. The Jews, however, have a great advantage over us: they have preserved and handed down communal memories, communal wisdom growing out of all the ups and downs of history. Thus they can pass on to each succeeding generation all the learning of the previous ones: this is how one lives with courage in a time of persecution, how one deals with potential enemies. The gay community, he points out, does not have this memory.

In part this is due to the fact that we may be born into the tribe, but we are not raised in it. Rarely do we have gay parents and grandparents who can pass the stories on to us. We do not bear descendants of our own, to whom we can relay what we have learned. And yet, we will have gay posterity, no matter who the children are conceived by; we will be, in the last analysis, the ancestors their tribal stories will evoke for them. Our ancestors were silent for too long. We must not be, for the sake of those who will come after us. We must begin to unearth, preserve, and pass on the tribal history, the wisdom of communal sufferings and triumphs.

The common history of faith that we share with the church at large tells only half the story. We can trace the calling of God's people in it, true, and insofar as we too are part of God's people, we can claim that story as our own. But there is a tremendous void within that story. Our names were not recorded, our presence not acknowledged, although there is no reason to doubt that we were present among God's people every step along the way. No one recorded what gay men and women said and did in Israel's flight to freedom, or on the morning of the Resurrection or the day of Pentecost. We do not even know the names of Jesus' gay disciples, or the lesbians who worshiped with the saints at Antioch. We can only trust that they were there.

The biblical story preserves for us the memory of how God called a people, raised them up as Yahweh's tribes. It does not recall for us how God called gay men and lesbians, though they were surely called, and surely answered. This, in particular, is an aching loss that we must somehow repair if we are to be spiritually whole. We must begin to know ourselves as God's gay people, God's gay tribe, called out to serve God in a unique and special way.

Here, then, must our work as lesbian and gay Christians begin: we must lay foundations to replace those that were buried in the silence of our communal history. We must tell the stories, weave the legends, paint the icons of another family of saints whose lives will give us light. Laws may be changed, church canons may be written, but until we can stand fast upon a spiritual foundation of our own shaping—and can pass it on to the gay children who will follow us—we will be strangers in the church, accepted or rejected at the whim of others, wearing second-hand garments someone else has chosen.

This is the first and most essential ministry of gay-to-gay, the only way in which, some day, we will be able to make God's gay children free.

So here is where I now propose to lay the first course of foundation stones. What can be found in the heart of our particular and often solitary journeys that marks us out as members of a family, a tribe who carry, one and all, a family likeness? How can we find in it the clear marks of God's presence working in our lives—not *despite* the fact that we are gay, but specifically *because* we are? How can we move out from the center of our individual and private stories to the creation of communal stories, communal language?

As one possible starting place, I would propose looking at the most formative and common experiences shared by gay men and lesbians, and recasting these in specifically spiritual terms.

Coming Out as Normative Experience

Coming out is the common heart of our particular journeys as gay men and women. For lesbian and gay Christians it is an inextricable element of our spiritual pilgrimage. For some it is the fulcrum of a spiritual conflict that estranges us from God or from the church, for others, the precipitating crisis that forces us into a deeper search for God. Almost never can the process be described as neutral.

How can we, then, as a people, talk about our spiritual lives without a reference to that one part of it which is, so often, its very genesis? How can we discuss "conversion," "commitment," "spiritual growth" without discussing this deepest and most personal experience of self-discovery and self-acceptance? Here, perhaps, is where our communal history must take a different route across the desert. Behind our stories and the stories of straight men and women's spiritual journeys may be one and the same prevenient grace, one Spirit touching us and drawing us along. But the straight disciple's story may or may not center on a sexual awakening. For God's gay people this is simply not the case. This, for good or ill, is the exact territory through which we must travel.

Here, then, is where I might begin our communal story, with this central, solitary journey, which is at the same time one of the deepest things we have in common: coming out.

Coming out is not peripheral to who we are as people or as Christians, rather it is the very form our spiritual journey takes, the means whereby God calls us out to be a people: God's gay tribe. It is the normative pattern of our spiritual growth.

Patterns of Spiritual Growth

There are observable patterns in the course of spiritual growth, patterns that, when fully realized, mark the development of those people we call "spiritually mature." We can discern this pattern in the lives of both the saints and spiritual revolutionaries (though their revolutions may have been entirely pacifistic ones). The details may differ; the exact arenas in which the stages of the journey are played out are always profoundly shaped by historical and cultural forces. But there are common threads that are always present.

PATTERNS OF SPIRITUAL GROWTH: COMING OUT AS SPIRITUAL JOURNEY

I.   Awakening or Conversion
1.   Spiritual awakening cannot be inherited, but must be self-discovered.
2.   This awareness sets us apart from others.
3.   It unmasks the bankruptcy of our previous lives.
4.   It impels us to some kind of action.

II.   Crossing the Wilderness, Facing the Shadows
1.   We are first stripped of all we have.
2.   We are forced to confront the demons.
3.   The desert journey discloses the God of the depths.
4.   It confers the power to prophesy.

III. Returning to the World
1.   The self emerges reintegrated or deeply changed.
2.   The sense of apartness takes on positive value.
3.   We speak with spiritual authority.
4.   We become agents of change.

The stories are entirely personal, their effects both social and communal. Spiritual growth takes place in an intensely individual and often solitary process. The Spirit works from within, but contrary to the conception popular in Western culture, there is no way in which the Spirit's work within is ultimately private. God of necessity transforms the world one person at a time. Each individual thus touched and transformed, though, acts much as a single cell behaves within an organism: transmitting life to every other cell. (The obverse is equally true: a single cell can ultimately infect and destroy an entire body.)

God acts, then, through the process of the solitary journey to transform the whole, and each man or woman who is pervious to the Spirit, open enough on some level to respond to the summons inward, becomes the bearer of a greater life for the body of the whole. This is why the life of a single man or woman can eventually touch and transform the conscience of an entire society. We are the conduits through which the Spirit pours out greater life into the world.

The inward journey is, paradoxically, the process whereby God first separates us, sets us apart, and then calls us out of our isolation into an identity that reaches beyond the limits of our skin. We become God's people, whose lives and destinies are forever bound up in the lives of others.

The pattern that has characterized the spiritual journeys of fully developed men and women can be stated in very simple terms. Its movement is essentially threefold:

1. Awakening or conversion.
2. Crossing the wilderness (facing the shadows).
3. Returning to the world.

Coming Out as Spiritual Journey

For gay men and women, this threefold pattern exists most immediately in that central journey we call "coming out." Its steps replicate the features of the classical spiritual pilgrimage. Too often, however, it is not fully recognized as a *spiritual* process by the gay man or woman living it out. This is due, in part, to two factors.

First, there is the Western cultural dichotomy between "body" and "spirit," or between "physical" and "spiritual." Nowhere is this split greater than in the area of sexuality, where popular religious culture is too apt to suspect anything sexual as being inherently sinful. Because coming out involves the discovery and experience of one's identity in a sexual context, all things connected with it are apt to be classified as "unspiritual" in the gay person's mind.

Second, our images of spiritual journey do not include the primary means and settings through which our self-discovery as gay persons often come. We can readily associate an experience that comes through inspirational reading, attending a church service, going on a silent retreat, and so on, as being spiritual. It is much, much more difficult for a gay person to see that a moment of insight that may have taken place in a gay bar is still fully "spiritual," no matter what its setting.

Nevertheless, when we are able to look beyond these cultural limitations, we can discover that inherent in the journey of coming out is the pattern of real spiritual development. For here, in the gay person's experience, is where the deepest wounds and fractures can exist, those very avenues through which the Spirit can touch even the most armor-plated self. Here is where we are most vulnerable and therefore most open to the Spirit. Here, then, is where God begins our transformation, amidst the pain, desire, and longing that accompany the process of coming out.

Awakening: Conversion to the Gay Identity

Substantial spiritual growth is not a simple progression of other growth
processes, the logical outcome of normal development, as routine and
predictable as learning to sit up or to talk. There is a radical point of
departure, some moment of turning in the life. It may be quiet in its
working, or as stunning as a lightning bolt. This is the point that we call
conversion, or awakening; an axial point at which the journey properly
begins. It is marked by several features:

1. *Spiritual awakening cannot be inherited, but must be self-discovered.*
Most of us inherit our primary religious convictions; they are absorbed
without thinking from the attitudes of parents and peers, or deliberately instilled by churches and Sunday schools. It is no secret to anyone
who has worked within a religious community of any kind that many
people never, in fact, feel called to go beyond whatever spiritual insight
they achieved in Sunday school.

In some individuals, however, temperament and circumstance (with a
large assist from the working of the Spirit) combine to force the person
beyond inherited modes of belief and thinking. The religious violence of
the seventeenth century and his own urgent desire for an assurance of
God's love impelled George Fox to look beyond the popular religiosity
of his day. The intense suffering Elizabeth Fry saw in the city slums, plus
her uneasy guilt at her own privileged and comfortable life, moved her
to reject the quietism of her family and go into the women's prisons to
minister and preach, much to the scandal of her neighbors.

The journey into real conversion always seems to start when men and
women arrive at the limits of the inherited forms of religious truth and
sense that there must be another truth beyond that, another level of life
to be lived, another way of knowing or of serving God. Awakening cannot be inherited: it is self-discovered.

This awakening or conversion is often the way in which God opens
up or breaks down barriers that have inhibited the work of the Spirit,
the coming of God's reign. In that sense, this awakening or conversion
challenges the limits of all inherited modes of belief or life.

For many gay men and lesbian women, the first great spiritual shock
comes with the recognition that we somehow cannot live within the
framework of inherited roles or gender expectations, that we must reject
what our entire culture takes as normal if we are to become who we truly
are. Parents do not urge us to grow up gay; schools do not provide us with
a list of gay men and women who shaped history; they seldom even name
gayness for us as children. We must always discover gayness for ourselves.

For many gay persons, it is the loneliness of that first tentative exploration of who we are, the forced departure from the safety of inherited

values, that makes us pervious to the Spirit at all. We cannot live lives of unthinking conformity, even if we want to. We have been started on a path that will inevitably lead us beyond the pale.

2. *This awareness sets us apart from others.*

Ordinary people find something excessive about any life bent wholly on the search for God. It is too challenging, too full of risk to be a comfortable prospect. The person who lives too close to God is dangerous. Historically, it has been seen as safer to set apart those who have that irresistible bent. Depending on the time and culture, they have been funneled into religious orders or sent off to serve in mission fields, in recognition that there was something "different" about them. The families of both Jesus and St. Francis were convinced they were unbalanced; St. Catherine's parents wore themselves out trying to make her be like other little girls. The "differentness" can be frustrated or rejected by the culture, but it cannot finally be eradicated.

The recognition that one is different, set apart in some way, is a common feature in the autobiographies of saints, but it is not confined there. A person's conviction that God has touched him or her in some special and profound way tends to surface early in life and is apparently indelible. The belief that God chooses, sets apart, and acts with radical particularity forms an essential part of both Jewish and Christian tradition.

How early does the recognition come for gay and lesbian persons? For many, it is there even before conscious memory begins. For me it was that morning I spoke of earlier, when little Stevie and I stood marooned in the center of the classroom, aware that we somehow did not fit the given categories. Despite the fact that I could neither name nor define the difference I knew about myself, I was very aware of it. It was years before I could frame the phrase (with an incredible sense of relief): "I am gay. That's what I am."

This early experience of being different becomes one of the very ways in which gay men and women are made open to God in the first place. It is not simply a sexual difference; it is a sense of differentness that goes as deep as we do and that bonds us invisibly into the company of all those, in every age, whom God has chosen, set apart, and claimed as a separate people.

3. *Conversion unmasks the bankruptcy of our previous lives.*

This is a powerful element in any spiritual awakening, as readily observed in ordinary Christians as it is in spiritual athletes. God opens our eyes or ears, and we suddenly see our lives with all their flaws and fractures. An ordinary person suddenly hears the gospel one Sunday morning and becomes aware that much of what he or she has lived for is inherently empty or meaningless. Something is missing; something is amiss. The desire for social standing, prestige, security, may suddenly appear unendurably narrow beside the imperative message of the gospel.

How much more bankrupt it seems to those who have invested years in trying to be someone they are not: the marriages too many of us make to try to force our lives into the "normal" pattern; the careers chosen to avoid admitting that our real love lies in some field too readily stereotyped as effeminate; the amount of time and energy we spend immersing ourselves in a round of frantic work or activity to still the voices inside. The stories come in all varieties. Their common feature is that, when we fully begin to accept our identity as gay, there is often a terrible recognition that our lives have been misplaced, misspent, misshapen.

Whatever the particular scenario, coming out throws a merciless spotlight on the unendurable reality of having lived a lie. It is an insight that we can never thereafter escape, even if we resist the motion to self-actualization. It is the price of spiritual awareness for anyone, whether straight or gay: we can never return to blissful ignorance.

4. It impels us to some kind of action.
A real revelation is not something that we grasp, but one that grasps us and will not let us go. It is played out not merely in the revolution it may create in the way we see the world, the way we think, the way we feel about ourselves, but it keeps up a relentless inner pressure until we let it move us, let it impel us into action. When circumstances do not permit us to act, we can wear our lives out in frustrated zeal or be driven into actual insanity. The prophet Jeremiah said it so aptly: "If I say, 'I will not mention him, or speak any more in his name,' then within me there is something like a burning fire shut up in my bones; I am weary with holding it in, and I cannot" (Jeremiah 20:9).

God does not open our eyes simply to teach us. Always, revelation has been the prelude to a life lived out in very different terms, a life spent acting out some great imperative of God's. Paul's blinding moment on the road to Damascus did not merely turn his hatred of the new Christian community into enlightened tolerance: its ultimate outcome was a life expended in preaching the gospel. God's word is heard with the ear, but enacted with the entire life.

In just the same way, to be gay is not simply to mentally or emotionally recognize one's nature: it implies a way of being in the world. We may struggle for months or even years to ignore this summons, to remain in our safe (if dishonest) lives. But we have no peace until we finally act on our knowledge.

This is the first stage of the journey, the identical path that saints and spiritual pioneers have walked. Gay men and women find themselves acting out this coming-out journey, with or without recognizing it as the fertile ground of spiritual growth. Part of reclaiming our spiritual identity as a people lies in consciously and deliberately articulating the spiritual dimension of this journey and recognizing it as the normative process of gay spiritual development.

Crossing the Wilderness, Facing the Shadows

We are the inheritors of a long tradition of desert spirituality. Both the Hebrew and Christian traditions recognize the desert—literally or symbolically—as that place where, separated from the safety of inherited but confining systems, undistracted by external diversions, the inner drama is played out. It is paradoxically the place of both exile and refuge, of loss and discovery. Whether it is the symbolic stage called the Dark Night of the Soul or Crossing the Sands, or the real-life flight into solitude practiced by the Desert Fathers and Mothers, it is the real crucible of emerging spirituality.

The moment of conversion may be supercharged with energy, dazzled with a sudden vision of what we are called to. There may be an intense and rapturous period of "honeymoon," as radical shifts take place in our vision and our personalities.

Inevitably, these are followed by a profound period of discontinuity, perhaps the natural consequence of those same drastic shifts. This is the stage of darkness or struggle, what is called very truly "crossing the sands alone." This stage, too, is marked by common features.

1. *We are first stripped of all we have.*
In the very act of stepping (or being impelled) outside the limits of inherited roles or traditions, we find ourselves unable to rely on things previously learned or valued. In that sense, we find ourselves stripped of the external supports that we have relied on in the past. In spiritual terms, this may create a terrifying sense that we are losing our comforting practices, or an even more terrifying sense that we are somehow challenging unassailable religious truths—even challenging God.

Moreover, it is not unusual for people who have achieved sudden new insight into the nature and call of God to find themselves at odds with their previous community, even to the point of being rejected by it. This is true even of those who are later called saints by that same community. St. Francis is just one example. The prophets of Israel, likewise, were revered when they were safely dead, but regarded as dangerous or treasonable while they lived.

This loss of external support is often an abrupt and cruel experience for gay men and women. Families may disown us, friends avoid us, and our churches condemn us as unspeakable sinners and abominations. We are completely beyond the pale, and we know it. The loss of family, particularly, may involve enormous grief and pain, an intense bereavement that we cannot even openly mourn. This is, for many gay people, the very thing which they have spent years trying to avoid: the fear that they will be treated like lepers, driven out of the community.

The desert experience is all the more intense because it is a solitary one. Frequently, the gay man or woman has not yet discovered gay community and is still struggling with the fear that he or she is "the only one." More often, it is the belief that God condemns or abhors the gay person that creates the sense of abandonment.

But the desert way is also the beginning of a journey to freedom. The children of Israel had to cross the wilderness before they entered into the land of promise; Jesus himself experienced the sense of complete abandonment at the crucifixion. Only in retrospect do we see the ways in which this period of desolation is in fact the very means whereby God strips away the old and prepares us for the new.

2. We are forced to confront the demons.
In the emptiness and silence of the desert place, we become aware of all the things we previously denied or avoided. We are stripped of habit and defense and may feel ourselves assaulted by all the things we had previously held at arm's length. In symbolic terms, we all have demons that we have to confront.

Our over-psychologized age is too apt to dismiss the struggles of an Antony or a Catherine of Siena as the sick projections of repressed and unbalanced personalities. Yet, however foreign the pictures of these demonic struggles may appear to us, they ring astonishingly true in modern terms, as well. We, too, have our demons, and the struggle with them is not any easier because we locate them inside ourselves, and not outside.

In one sense, it is quite true that the struggle is a struggle with the self, particularly with the deepest and most rigorously repressed parts of the self. We all possess a shadow side, the disowned and often hated parts of our own natures that we cannot claim as ours. They are our indefatigable companions in exile, the shadows that dog our steps across the sands. We cannot outrun them, and in the shelterless place of exile, they may seem to spring out at us with merciless fury.

For gay men and women, coming out may push long-repressed emotions to the surface, and we may have to wrestle with the depths of our own anger or sense of betrayal, or an overwhelming rage at the injustice of our lives. There may be grief too deep for words, and bitterness that we have carried all our lives. It is devastating to admit that we can hate, that we can want revenge on those who have hurt or rejected us, that we cannot master or control our feelings.

A young gay man, whose spiritual desert was his three-year struggle with AIDS, wrote: "I don't know that I'm winning my fight with my emotions, but at least I know that they're *mine*. It's not my dad's anger and rejection that I'm struggling with, but my own. The struggle gets harder all the time, and that discouraged me a lot at first. Now I know it's because I'm getting stronger in my ability to face my feelings and resist them pushing me around. I can't make Dad accept me or forgive me, but I am really struggling with my own unwillingness to forgive him."

It is sometimes difficult to affirm this as an indispensable part of our spiritual growth, but the fact is, we achieve the wholeness God intends for us not by rejecting what we feel are unacceptable parts of ourselves, but by ultimately incorporating and transforming them. We cannot emerge from the desert place until we have at least begun the confrontation. Coming out merely brings us to the threshold of the wrestling ground.

3. The desert journey discloses the God of the depths.

Stripped of our supports and pushed beyond the limits of our own resources, we are at the same time pushed beyond our images of God. This may be experienced as a profound sense of abandonment or loss or a "dazzling darkness" in which God is hidden from us. Even people well-grounded in a religious tradition may, at this point, find their sense of God totally evaporating.

It is only when we have been brought to the very edge of our resources, know the utter desolation of our outcast state, that we are either exhausted enough to let go of our hold or desperate enough to throw ourselves into the deeper emptiness that lies below the surface emptiness of the desert journey: the abyss of God.

At the bottom of this great fall, we become aware of God not in a way we previously understood, but in a new way altogether: the God of the depths, who shares the empty places with us. In Christian terms, it is only when we have fully become the outcast that we know the God who comes not only to seek out the outcast, but to share the exile.

This is the end of terror and the beginning of real healing. This is the point at which God is, for all time, changed in our eyes: no longer the condemning judge or the threatening parent, but the one who has chosen to share our abandonment.

For gay persons, in particular, this stage of coming out may be as earth-shaking as their recognition of being gay was in the first place. For as our image of God as terrorist and judge begins to shatter, it takes with it the enculturated guilt and fear that many gay men and women carry, the conviction that God condemns us for our very natures.

From this moment on, we can begin to recognize that condemning families, friends, and churches do not speak for God. Rather, God joins us and upholds us in our struggle with them. God ceases to be the enemy.

Significantly, this discovery does not spell the conclusion of the desert journey, but merely its turning point. The traveler may have to retrace the long road that led into the wilderness before emerging from it. But the essential fact is that, even without being restored to his or her former community, the traveler is no longer alone.

Perhaps more subtly, but just as indelibly, this experience of God's solidarity with our lostness creates a bond that reattaches us to others in a different way. For now, just as we have experienced God's willingness to share our exile and be present with us, we become more and more aware that we are bound to every other outcast and are called by God to walk with them as God has walked with us.

It is not insignificant that gay men and women who have traveled this road so often become committed to the causes of peace and social justice. The desert is a sensitizing place, in which we learn to feel others' lostness as our own and are impelled to act in solidarity with other outcasts. Coming out is simultaneously coming in to solidarity with others.

4. *Crossing the wilderness confers the power to prophesy.*
The image of the desert as "the womb of prophets" is a deeply embedded image in our spiritual heritage. Like the image of wrestling with the demons, however, it is likely to embarrass North Americans, who associate the word *prophet* with New Age futurists or the ultra-fundamental millennialists who almost daily warn us that the end is near. Even its use within the Christian community (as in the adjective *prophetic*) is perhaps misleading in this context, as it may or may not take forms we associate with prophetic ministry.

It might be nearer to the mark to put it in another way: the desert journey makes us, finally, truth-tellers.

It is intimately bound up in the twofold revelation that has taken place: God is not the source of our pain, but its companion, and our exile is not merely a unique and individual experience, but the very place where we are bound most closely to the fractured lives of others.

The desert journey is also powerfully informed by having wrestled with our interior demons, that stripping away of our illusions about our own natures. We can name the shadows once we have the courage to accept them as a part of our own natures. In that sense, we can never again entirely externalize them, never quite disown them or attribute them to others.

Only after our time in the desert can we name with clarity the lies, the evasions, and the pains that drove us to the journey in the first place, including the lies and evasions that were of our own making. Only then can we speak fearlessly, in one sense having nothing more to lose. It is at this point in the classical journey that the emergent traveler begins to dare an open challenge to previously sacrosanct ideas and religious systems. This is sometimes dramatically visible, as in the case of Luther or George Fox. Or it may simply be the inner process whereby one is ready to reject forever all those things that did not survive the desert crossing.

For the lesbian or gay man, this stage of coming out may be signaled by an increasingly open and vocal lifestyle, ready to confront or challenge homophobic relatives or civil codes. In quieter, but no less forceful ways, it may be articulated by *living* the truth of who we are. The point is: we know the truth, and must, in some way or another, express it. Like the prophetic figures of our heritage, gay men and women may, at this point, feel an overwhelming sense of being called to speak the truth both to and on behalf of others.

In many ways, the desert journey is the seminal experience, the matrix in which the shape of the mature self will be cast; what we become retains the marks of the furnace forever. This may be the singular experience that signals spiritual rebirth, or a struggle that must be repeated many times within our lifetime. Its relative duration may be short and quite intense, or it may stretch on for years. There is no way of predicting this, once we have crossed the threshold of the wilderness, and that too is a necessary risk.

The "desert journey" is not, after all, a mere literary convention that describes this stage of growth in terms of threatening and lonely places. This is a dangerous journey: no one undertakes it who can possibly avoid it. There are real possibilities that one may not make it out the other side. This is one of the reasons religious communities hedge the journey around with disciplines and inherited traditions: they are sometimes the only safeguards we have. For this reason, too, whoever has come through the journey must finally share their knowledge with others: this is where communal memories must not be lost.

Returning to the World: Integration and Emergence

The transition from the desert journey back to "ordinary life" may be as cataclysmic and abrupt as the descent into the wilderness, or it may come gradually, even gently. In some spiritual biographies, we find a kind of curious reluctance to emerge: the empty places have become the place of refuge rather than of exile, the barrenness a kind of exquisite simplicity.

The meaning of this movement becomes apparent only after it is left behind. The desert exists to deliver us to another destination, the dark night to prepare us for another light. At some moment, the traveler is summoned to return to life, either by the reawakening of the energies no longer needed for a struggle or by the very movements of daily life.

The self that emerges, however, will not be the same one who originally entered the wilderness. It will be characterized by several features:

1. The self emerges reintegrated or deeply changed.
There is a saying often used of silent prayer: *Nothing can be brought to the presence of God and remain unchanged.* This may be equally true of the wilderness sojourn. No one can pass through it and emerge the same as they went in. The extent of the change will often be in direct proportion to the depth of the struggle and the length of the journey. Paradoxically, the more shattering the experience, the more whole we are on coming out of it. This is not to be wondered at: part of what has fueled the struggle are the deep divisions, conflicts, and fracture lines within the personality and worldview.

We may, in fact, continue living in the same town, family, and church community, but the relationship to it, and above all, the perception of it will have changed. (It is often astonishing to gay men and women to discover, at this point, that they can go on relating to families that still do not accept them as gay, but without the earlier sense of conflict or bereavement. It is not the situation that has changed, but both the point from which we view it and the eyes through which we see it.)

In the breaking up of what has often been a deeply conflicted view of life, the pieces are reordered into something closer to coherence: outgrown beliefs and values have been left behind, and more powerful and focused ones achieved.

In part, this is the natural result of being able to drop the camouflage, the personas gay men and women often have to adopt in order to survive or remain undetected. To say that what emerges is much closer to the original self, before the process of disguise began, would be to oversimplify. The self that emerges is not what would have been achieved if no disguises had been worn: it is a new creation.

We may, in fact, become aware of qualities and gifts in ourselves that were not previously evident: of confidence or courage, compassion or the willingness to make decisions. This is not a mere subjective phenomenon. It is observable by others, often long before we see it for ourselves.

The essential thing is this: this is the point at which our coming out becomes real. That is, we are actually *out*. There is life after the abyss, and after all the losses, and it rests upon a different center. It is not simply the resolution of our previous conflicts or the overcoming of our previous problems. The transformation has, in fact, been spiritual.

2. The sense of apartness takes on positive value.
The fact that life may now resume a quieter, more normal tenor does not mean that we are effortlessly reintegrated into our previous setting, reharmonized with our milieu. The apartness may actually have deepened; if it

is not more visible, it is at least more consciously recognized. The essential difference is that now, perhaps for the first time, this apartness is no longer negative, no longer a source of pain or anxiety ("What's wrong with me? Why can't I be like other people?"). It is a conscious recognition that there is a profound rightness in being different; it has a value and a meaning.

This is the permanent outcome of our naked and defenseless meeting with the God of the depths. We have, in some way or another, been known right to our depths, and this will mark us forever. In the final stages of the desert sojourn, we are likely to have a vivid sense that the entire experience was finally God's way of meeting with us. We have been drawn apart precisely to be set apart: marked in some way as God's own. This apartness, paradoxically, at one and the same time breaches the walls of our separateness: we have been set apart *for* some reason, *for* God, *for* some calling.

This may be the first real peace we have in accepting our nature. We are gay, and this will always make us different. But the differentness is at the same time a sense of specialness: our gayness is a gift, a quality that adds to who we are, that gives us something more than we would have had if we had not been created gay. This is a differentness that can be lived with pride, a mark of how deeply and how fully God loves us.

Here, perhaps, is the most striking thing we find in dialogue with straight Christians. Even when they totally affirm our being full members of the church, or fully God's children, it is often on the basis of "You're really just like us, except for who attracts you sexually." I have yet to meet a spiritually mature gay man or woman who agrees with that. Even without a language to articulate what it is that sets us apart from our straight brothers and sisters, we who have been to the depths of our own natures come away with an awed and overwhelming sense of gratitude: how incredible to think that God should have loved us so much that we were given this enormous gift, this mark, this otherness!

When this sense of apartness is paired with the experience of God's solidarity with us, and ours with each other, it becomes the understanding that being set apart finds its real meaning only when we are also called into the midst of God's full household, to occupy a special role in adding to the life of God's people, the body of Christ.

3. We speak with spiritual authority.
There is something indelible about the experience of having every outside support or comfort stripped away, a bone-deep imprint that remains with us forever. In part, it is the lesson we have learned: that external security is at best completely transient or fragile. It was swept away before; it could be, easily, again.

Even more profound than that, the spiritually seasoned man or woman now must look beyond inherited or given systems for the sources of authority. That is, one is no longer forced to locate spiritual authority in external sources, to look for approval, to seek permission. What is often the most striking thing about the returning exile is how often he or she can speak and act with a compelling and convincing air of spiritual authority, based on no visible or ordinary source.

This is not, in any sense, the ordinary notion that one *has* authority. In fact, travelers emerging from the sands are often acutely aware that they possess nothing at all but what is within them; everything else has gone. In that sense, they are not fooled by the thought that they now have authority. Instead, there is a deep conviction that they can speak or act *with* authority, which is a very different thing.

The roots of this simultaneous sense of empty-handedness and confidence lie in our encounter with the God of the depths. We have had a deep and direct experience of utter powerlessness, and an equally compelling meeting with the source of all authority and power. The direct and personal nature of this encounter confers confidence: having heard with our own ears and seen with our own eyes, we cannot thereafter defer to second-hand accounts. It is not a matter of rational decision; it is a simple fact of life. An accomplished musician can perform a piece with masterful authority, but the performance is based on the ability to have caught and heard what the music itself insists on. It is, in fact, an utmost deference to the authority of the composition itself. Just so with the returning traveler.

It is the experience of God, the sense that we have glimpsed some overwhelming truth, that is the basis of this spiritual authority. It cannot be conferred. It can only be recognized. This, particularly, can be seen in those lesbians and gay men who have begun to grasp to some extent the truth of who they are. It is not opinions that they assert; it is the direct expression of the amazing truth they have been shown.

4. *We become agents of change.*

Just as nothing can be brought to God's presence and remain unchanged, whatever emerges from God's presence will inevitably change everything it touches. The change is not necessarily brought about by conscious action, or deliberate attempt. The power to change others operates on a different level altogether. Bringing a fire into a room will change the whole room's temperature, by the very fact of the fire simply being itself. This is, perhaps, one reason why we fear the prophet who emerges from the desert: we instinctively feel the reflected heat and sense that, if we draw too close, we will be scorched.

The drastic freedom of the emergent self may, by its very nature, open doors of change for others. This may be as simple as our inability to act out older scripts, which forces those around us into unusual and new reactions. It may, likewise, be the greater freedom that the desert journey finally engendered, which in turn permits a greater freedom to all others.

An even deeper level, however, is especially important for gay men and women to acknowledge and recognize. We are members of a body, parts of one another's lives, for good or ill. Whatever we experience becomes a part of our collective and communal being.

Our private anger, bitterness, and grief are not contained within the silence of our own minds and hearts, but leaven the whole. Likewise, whatever freedom, healing, and forgiveness we experience within our own lives also become part of the shared life. Seen in this light, even what we cannot verbally articulate inevitably brings change into the life of every person who shares that communal life with us.

Our solitary journeys into spiritual wholeness as gay men and women are not private affairs: they are social and communal acts, whose purpose is the spiritual transformation of the gay community, which in turn has the challenge of helping the larger community of Christianity to which we belong to continue its own long journey of transformation.

BILL: HANGING OUT WITH THE CHURCH

The Dangerous Oasis

To borrow the desert image that M. R. uses: here you are, making your way across the desert, and you've just about drunk the last of your water. Finally you crawl to the top of the next dune, and there, on the horizon, you see a steeple. You don't know if it's a peaceful oasis or a gang of robbers. The church can be an unknown commodity in that regard. It can be really bad, or really good, or—most likely—somewhere in between.

So one of the things we have to talk about when we talk about gay and lesbian spirituality is how we deal with the church, how we deal with organized religion. It's not the same thing as spirituality. This a very important thing to understand. Spirituality is our interaction with God, and therefore our interaction with God's creation, including ourselves, and the way we've been created. That encounter with God creates an assurance that we have really, somewhere in our lives, touched foot to solid ground. And that is confirmed in the message of the gospel—the assurance that God is love, that God is not dismayed by our weaknesses, that God is, in fact, always working with us, that God has created us for love, and that God will go on asking us for our love in return. Together, the gospel and our own experience form the bedrock of our spirituality.

To a degree, we learn about this tradition of spirituality from the church. The church is the institution that very kindly maintains the spiritual tradition that undercuts it—or, at least undercuts its pretensions to perfect knowledge of God. Preserving this tradition is the great thing about the church, even though much of the time it does it without knowing what it's doing. Michael Malone's novel *Handling Sin*—a terribly funny book—comments on a church in South Carolina that had a gallery where the masters generously let their slaves sit and overhear the message about the Exodus! The church does that all the time with all sorts of people. It lets people in on God's secrets without intending to. And then sometimes the church gets very upset and tries to take what it's said back—tries to say, "Oh, we didn't mean *you*. That's just for people like us. There's a different message for you. God loves us, but you're bad. God loves us, but you're a slave. Oh, God will try to love you if you're an obedient slave, or if you try very hard to be heterosexual just like us, or if you'll at least feel very, very bad because you can't be just like us. But don't imagine that you really *belong* here." So the church, historically, has been both the bearer of the good news and its betrayer.

It's easy to understand, then, why many gay and lesbian people who have come out turn away decisively from the church and don't want to have anything to do with it again. The church has often tried to prevent us from acknowledging who we really are or insisted on raising a barrier between us and God. And yet, some of us haven't quite been able to turn our backs on the church. Sometimes I wish I could, as it might make life simpler and less quarrelsome. But I'm still here. God seems to be determined that I will not turn loose of this relationship. I sometimes think that not figuring out I was gay until my late thirties was an awkward kind of grace. Perhaps God wanted me to have a strong identification as a Christian and an Episcopalian before letting the two identities come into conflict with each other. That way, I wouldn't easily be able to shed either one of them. It wouldn't be the only time I've known God to play that sort of trick.

Those of us who have been called to stay in communion with the church have to think a bit about how to live with it. It will be worth the trouble only if we can help raise up once again in our generation the centrality of the good news of the gospel instead of saying, "Oh, yes, business as usual." It's not that the church is any worse than other human institutions. Over a span of centuries, it probably averages out with government and education and the rest. It's not the worst institution, but it's a human institution all the same. On the principal of total depravity, you have to expect that every human institution can be turned to evil just as easily as to good—maybe more easily. There may be a principle of spiritual entropy at work here that says evil is the default option. Still, what are the chances that the spiritual riches of the gospel would still be available to us without the fallible human community that is charged with maintaining and communicating them?

Living with—or in Spite of—the Church

So how do we go about living with the church while maintaining a dry-eyed, hard-headed view of what the church really is? How do we comprehend both the good things it can offer us and the bad things it can do to us? Well, of course, churches differ in their precise details, and we all face different situations in terms of our denominations. Often it's the local congregation that's the real key for us. Congregations, even in the same denomination, can vary enormously. A great many lesbian and gay people have managed to find places where we can feel at least somewhat welcome. But it can be a long and precarious search, and we always have the question of exactly how to live with the church. If God is going to insist that we do that, *how* do we do it?

I think the key here—and I hate to say this because I don't particularly enjoy it—is developing a certain degree of maturity. We need to move beyond the kind of sweeping dualistic judgment that says, "If it isn't completely good, it's completely bad"—the sort of binary opposition that is our preferred human mode of thinking. Some anthropologists say this mindset is almost inescapable, but I don't believe that. We can recognize our dualistic tendencies and still begin to develop a more nuanced view of the world. In fact, that's one of the things that growing up is all about. At times it's terribly frustrating, because it means that life is never going to be *all* good. (As a consolation, it probably means that it's never going to be all bad, either, though it can get pretty close to it at times.)

Many of us started our life journey struggling with such binary oppositions. We began with "Gay is bad," and then we moved to "Gay is good." And we'd like to stay there, but after you've lived as a gay person with other gay people for five or six years, you begin to think, "Well, maybe it's less clearcut than that; maybe gay people—like everybody else—can be good at times and bad at times." The same individual, in fact, can be good at times and bad at times. Being gay isn't any guarantee of being enlightened or generous or understanding—even understanding of other people who are just now going through what you've already gone through. In the same way, the church may have started off as a good thing and then invented its own favorite ways of being a bad thing. But, over all, the church has both good elements and bad. And even those are not fixed; they change even as we interact with them. Don't expect to settle into the church as if it were a warm bath. On the other hand, there are some gifts here that are not so easily found elsewhere.

One important element in our accommodation to the church is to remember that the church is much less than it often wants to appear. The church is constantly getting itself confused with God in a whole variety of ways. The favorite way in American culture is to say, "The Bible is the word of God, and it tells you literally everything you should do—except of course you're not educated enough or pure enough or pious enough to understand that, so I'll tell you." The Bible is the "preserved word of God," and it gives you directions about everything. I grew up in the Bible Belt, and even though I wasn't raised Fundamentalist, no one could escape knowing the way they operated. Fundamentalists always claim that they read the Bible literally. And they do, when it suits them. When it doesn't suit them, they don't. It's strange how the plainest statement in the Bible can become a great mystery that we don't understand yet, and so you mustn't take it too seriously. "Wives, obey your husbands"—yes, that seems clear to the Fundamentalist; but "Judge not lest ye be judged"—that's another matter altogether. Why, the world just wouldn't work at all if we couldn't judge others. So whatever Jesus meant by that, he didn't mean it in the simple, literal sense.

Fundamentalists cover up by accusing everyone else of reading the Bible selectively. After all, people say the best defense is a good offense. Accuse others of your own sins, and they won't have time to notice that that's what you're doing yourself. We need to do exactly that: *notice*. Notice when the church is overstepping its bounds, when it has been far too sure of itself for any human institution, when it is using its religious status to oppress people instead of giving them hope. And then remember that this isn't really what the church is for.

Where Does the Church Come from?

The church is not God. In fact it's a long way from being God. Where does the church come from? There are a few hints about it in the Gospels, but really not much. There's nothing to suggest that Jesus founded the church in all its organizational complexity. He was content with a ragtag group of followers. The church certainly isn't something that Jesus brought down out of heaven or established in perfect form once and for all. The church is something created by human beings who heard the gospel, who were brought together by the gospel, and who began thinking "Well, what does that mean for our lives? How can we help one another understand it? How can we keep this encounter with God fresh in our memories?"

You see this process going on in the letters of Paul. It's clear, when you read them, that the communities Paul founded didn't have a complete set of agreed doctrines, weren't too sure of what the standards of behavior should be, and had only a minimal notion of how to organize their congregations. At the end of First Corinthians, Paul says something like, "Oh, by the way, take people like Stephanas seriously, because he was one of the first converts in the area, and besides, he and his household have been very hospitable to the church. So do what they say." (16:15–16) As soon as you read that, you realize that there was, at that point, no organized church government in Corinth. Paul hadn't left anybody in charge. It hadn't *occurred* to him to leave anybody in charge. Only after all kinds of disruption within the Corinthian church did he begin to realize that there had to be some kind of structure. It was invent as you go.

Now, this is true of all religion, however much it tries to deny it. The fundamental thing—the point where it all begins—isn't religion. The fundamental thing is people encountering God—or rather, God encountering people, for it always happens God's way and not ours. It's not under our control. Perhaps you've had the experience of some truly remarkable moment of encounter with God in the mountains. For me, it usually happens in a place where there is desert and running water. I remember it happening the first two times I visited Zion National Park in southern Utah, at the Hanging Gardens just inside the Narrows there. And then, on my third visit, nothing special! It was still a place of great beauty, and I enjoyed being there. But the encounter with God that I had thought must be routine there turned out not to be.

I don't think God wants us to settle into an expectation that we can compel God's presence by going to a certain place, by saying a certain prayer, by following a certain rite. Why? Because God is always God, and we're not. And the church is not. And the Bible is not. God is always God. Yet, God does, graciously, seek out encounter with us; and for those of us who are gay or lesbian, one place the encounter often happens is in the process of our self-discovery, our coming out. That's important; it's worth hanging onto. We can all learn from other people's experience of God. But if you've got to make a choice between your own experience of God's grace and what somebody tells you about God, you must, like the blind man in John's Gospel, hang onto your own experience. At the same time, we know that our own experience isn't always perfectly clear, that we don't understand it perfectly, that we need to go deeper. And so what do we do? We talk to one another. We try to find others who may have a glimmer of what this was about for us and may be able to shed a new light on it from a different angle, the angle of their own experience of God, so that it will become clearer for us.

We all serve one another as priests, simply by virtue of our being human. We all stand in the presence of the Holy, in the presence of God. Maybe some of us pay more attention than others, but we're all there, each with a unique vantage point. God is looking for us all. God isn't leaving anybody out. And so we expect, intuitively, that we'll be able to help one another. We'll be able to find out more about our own experience by comparing notes, by hearing the experience of others, by seeing how other people interpret both their experience and ours.

We receive the gifts of priestly service from others, and we give them to others. Sometimes we're not even aware that we're doing it. Because it's such a basic human thing, we may not think it's anything important or unusual. In fact, it's sometimes just part of the ordinary business of life. Years ago, a colleague and I began teaching together at a new place, and we were both perplexed at times by our experience there. After faculty meetings, we would go out and have a beer and say, "What the hell was going on in there today?" Some fierce battle was being waged, but we couldn't quite figure out what had triggered it. (Eventually we concluded that, whatever it was, it had happened at least fifteen years before, but was still being fought over.) The beers and postmortem were a kind of priesthood—a couple of people helping each other understand reality. Perhaps it wasn't a deep issue of spirituality that was at stake (though I wouldn't want to shortchange the importance of community dynamics in the workplace). But the same process carries over into all aspects of life. When we're specifically talking about our encounters with God, we definitely want to call it priesthood.

Priesthood is a lot like the encounter with God itself, in that we don't have control of it. A few of the valuable things I've been told in my life actually came from people who were not meaning to be kind and helpful. They came from people who were meaning to do me some harm, or even from people who weren't talking to me. Some fragment of overheard conversation has occasionally turned a light on for me. This priesthood is not something that you can get all organized and under control. That doesn't make it less important, but it does leave you wondering how to make it more accessible.

Religion as Scale Model

What do we do about this priesthood as human beings? We have to have some way of talking about our experience of God and priesthood, because they're central and revelatory for us; yet, at the same time, they're sufficiently fleeting and unpredictable that we can't quite get a grip on them. We've got words like *God*, but how do we define it? We can define *chair*. We can show people chairs and agree on which things are chairs and which are not chairs—which are, say, tables or stools. But how do we define *God*? Somehow we have to create a language that will enable us to talk with one another about undefinable things. It will have to be a symbolic language, a kind of model of the whole process of meeting the Holy. So we create religion as a kind of scale model of our encounters with the Holy, and it gives us a language for our priestly ministrations to one another. It's tremendously useful. I don't know how we would do without it. We'd have no language at all for sharing our experience of God without the religious model.

The religious model even includes a model of priestly ministries in the form of ordained or sacramental priests and other ministers. The point of ordaining someone is not for the rest of us to be able to say, "Okay, there's the priest. I don't have to be one now." The point is to say, "Oh, that's right. That's who we are. We're priests." Like religion in general, the church's ordained priesthood is a kind of secondary formation, a scale model. The fundamental human priesthood is the one that goes on all the time among us, even when we're not conscious of it.

Religion, then, when it's functioning well, can be a very useful thing. But it's like everything human. It can be turned to evil uses. Sometimes it seems as if the corruption of the best turns out to be the worst. When religion goes bad, it goes really bad. Different traditions have their own preferred modes of doing that. I think the preferred mode in my own Anglican tradition is to get extremely boring and stuffy—and rather rigid about anything that isn't quite the way it was in grandmother's time. Most of American Protestantism prefers to wave the Bible and invoke the wrath of God. Other traditions have their own preferred modes. The church doesn't need any particular excuse to slide into these modes; it's an everpresent temptation. But sometimes this self-protective tendency in the church is a response to fear, and one thing that is apt to terrify the church is genuine spiritual experience.

Reawakening the Church

The church starts resting on its laurels, and thinking that, as long as we've got enough people or endowments to pay the bills, everything is fine. God is in heaven and should stay there. God should stay on the throne and not go running around the marketplace. The church is doing okay, and all's right with the world. The last thing the church wants to have show up at such times is genuine spiritual experience. Francis of Assisi, for example, was viewed with great suspicion. It was a real task for him to convince the hierarchy that they didn't need to shut him down. Teresa of Avila and John of the Cross both came within an inch of being thrown to the Inquisition. And the Wesleys encountered equally grave suspicions in the Anglican church, though fortunately they had no Inquisition to worry about. Neither of the Wesleys apparently wanted to leave Anglicanism, but the church was so frightened of what it called "enthusiasm" that it just couldn't accommodate their movement. The church is seldom really comfortable with live spiritual experience. Gay and lesbian people aren't the first to experience the problem.

We should probably expect, in our relationship with the church, that the mere fact we've been meeting with God or that God's been meeting with us, the mere fact that we've heard the good news in some new and vivid way, isn't necessarily going to endear us to the institution that provides us the language for talking about it. That doesn't mean the situation's hopeless. It just means that you find your priests wherever you find them. You find people who have heard the good news, who have been surprised by the good news—often quite against their will. And, in conversation with these people, the church starts to come to life again—sometimes quite against its will. Within the church, you can at least hope to find people who know the language of the good news. Perhaps it will come alive for them anew. Perhaps we will help it come alive for them.

For our own spiritual safety, then, we need to remember that the church is just the church and the Christian religion is just the Christian religion. Very useful, very valuable, and also very dangerous. We have to swear our primary allegiance to the God who has encountered us in our own lives, to the God who has somehow made the good news of Jesus come alive for us again in the context of our lives. The church needs that. It needs us at least as much as we need the church. We're not the only people who are encountering the gospel in our time, not at all. But the church needs all sorts of people who have heard God's good news so that the life of the Spirit comes back into the church.

This doesn't necessarily mean the church will *want* us, but it needs us. We have to understand that what we are bringing to the church out of the fruits of our lives is essential, if not always welcome. We can't look at the church simply as a parent who knows it all, as a big brother or big sister who will always encourage us and support us. Instead, we have to look at the church as an instrument of humanity in its effort to find a way to talk about its encounter with God—and also as the great temptation that goes along with that. It might seem much easier if the church *were* God. Then everything would be predictable, and we wouldn't have to worry about where the real God, that great and loving Power who will never abide strictly by the rules, will show up next. But it won't work. Thank God!

So the church is not God. Religion is not the same thing as the encounter with God. The church and religion can be tremendously useful. They can provide language, create contexts for priestly conversation, and celebrate our shared experience of grace. But they also carry with them a great temptation and a great danger. There's a reason why you don't know whether that steeple you see on the horizon is a quiet oasis or a den of robbers. Even after you've gone on in and taken your first drink at the water hole, you still may not know. For the truth is that human beings, including ourselves, can't be permanently categorized. We're all, ourselves included, still involved in the process of deciding whether this is going to be a peaceful oasis or a robbers' den. The church isn't all good or all bad—and neither are we.

The Need for Community

A second thing we need to remember, in the effort to get past simple binary oppositions, is that we humans are social and cultural beings. This is true right from infancy. Studies indicate that babies who are not picked up and handled and talked to don't thrive, even if they are given the perfect diet and all the other physical requisites. Babies are, in a certain sense, not fully human yet—they are brought into full humanity by the ministry of other human beings. Even in our adult years, we still need this sort of fostering. We need the people around us to verify to us who we are, to help us change when we need to change, to help us find courage when we need to dig in our heels and say no. We never get past the point of needing one another. We live in a culture which assumes that the individual is fundamental. And gay and lesbian people have particular reason to know how important it is to be the people we are and not merely live out the social roles assigned to us by others. But we can't ignore the other side. We are fundamentally social creatures.

There's a difficult balance that we're constantly trying to strike here. If you have ever lived through a period in your work environment when someone, particularly someone in authority, was behaving in an antisocial way, you will know how tricky this is. A community is far more than just the sum of its parts. With bad leadership, people don't just continue doing what they can do. They get nervous. They start second-guessing themselves. They back off. Eventually, many will disappear altogether if the problem goes on long enough. Maybe you just want to get on with your job, but without a community that can honestly affirm what you're doing as part of a larger whole, that can become difficult. And most of us are not happy with merely retreating into ourselves, because it leaves a gaping absence. I've found, in such situations, that I just can't figure out a way to be human without a functional community. Sometimes we don't notice how deeply we're involved in our communities, but it's true for us anyway. And the time when we really find it out is when the community goes bad. Then we realize how much we've lost.

None of this is to imply that we can replace the individual with the community any more than we can replace the community with the individual. Human life is all about the interchange between those two. Different cultures may balance the two differently, but all human life involves a moving back and forth in conversation between those two poles. We have responsibilities to the communities of which we are a part; we also have responsibilities to ourselves. The balance we're seeking is implied in the recognition that God loves each of us as much as anybody on the planet—not more than anybody else on the planet, but certainly not one iota less. And therefore, I presume, God thinks that we ought to take ourselves seriously in both our individual and our communal aspects. Of course, by "seriously" I don't mean "solemnly." Human beings were not built, physically or spiritually, to keep long faces all the time. If we're going to take humanity seriously, our propensity for play and delight has to come in there somewhere, too. I mean simply that our own importance as individuals doesn't yield automatically to the importance of the community—and the importance of the community doesn't yield automatically to our individual importance. God loves it all.

Staying In and Coming Out

Being present to our church community, as gay and lesbian people, will eventually involve coming out. I've heard John McNeill, one of the pioneers of gay Christian spirituality, say on more than one occasion that it's very important to come out: It's important for your spiritual integrity. It's important for what it can do in and for your community. It's important for what it can do for other gay people who may not have reached that point yet. At the same time, McNeill also insists that it's important not to get too far ahead of yourself. There will almost always be some tension involved in taking this step, at times even a well-placed trepidation. But the desire we sometimes feel, early in the coming-out process, to do the most radical thing imaginable and get it all over with is often not the best thing. We need to have some sense that we have the spiritual resources to go forward from that point, even if much of our community responds badly.

As we live with and in the church, we may receive gladly those moments when the community does sustain us, but we also recognize that we can't just turn the whole job over to the church. We have to make conscious provision of who and what we need to sustain us spiritually. We need to think about how we're going to be fed, as well as what we're going to give to others. In every community, we expect both to give and to receive. In healthy communities, those remain, over the long term, in some kind of balance with each other. We don't divide the group into those who are expected to give, give, give and those who are free to do nothing but take. And our spiritual lives as individuals require some such balance in their interchange with others. Jesus did not say—nor does the passage in Leviticus 19:18 that he quotes say—"Love your neighbor instead of yourself." The commandment is "Love your neighbor as yourself." Love both, with as close an equality as you can manage. And leave your neighbor free to show the same kind of love toward you.

So the first thing for lesbian and gay people to remember about the church is that it's not God. The church can be very useful as a religious model to help us think and talk about our encounters with God. It can also be very dangerous when it tries to substitute itself for God. But it's not God. We, of all people, must be very careful not to grant it that power.

The second thing is to remember that all human life functions on this spectrum between the community and the individual. Neither can sustain itself alone. In order to be useful either to ourselves or to the community we have to keep the traffic moving. We have to keep moving back and forth along that line, taking our own lives and experience seriously and also looking for the help that others can give us in understanding them and finding the courage and hope to live them well. And in our personal lives, we need to seek a balance of giving and receiving, of loving and being loved.

The Giver and the Gift

Finally, one other thing that we need to keep in mind is that the gospel is a gift, a grace. We didn't receive the good that we have received from God because we earned it. We received it because God is good, and God saw that this was the moment for us to receive this gift. The early Christians emphasized forgiveness very strongly as the foundation of their faith. This wasn't because they were uniquely sinful. It was because, if God gives grace to all of us by means of *forgiveness*, not because we deserved it, then we can never fall through the safety net. We may, of course, say to ourselves, "I don't need that much forgiveness, and if God wants to go around forgiving people, I could give him a list." And we may be right. But it's okay. What it means is that God isn't waiting for us to deserve love. God loves us right now, warts and all. And even if we acquire new warts later on, God isn't going to quit loving us.

Now, does this mean that anything goes, that God doesn't care about who or what we are becoming? Not at all. God cares a great deal. God rejoices with us in every moment when our lives become more coherent, truer, more transparent to the holy, more joyful, more loving, more generous. How could God not rejoice in all that? God loves us, and is therefore delighted in everything good that we are able to accomplish. But it's not the starting point; it's the not the minimum required for admission. We don't have to earn God's love.

In fact, if we want to earn God's love, it's too bad, because we're too late. We already have it. We have all the love God has to give. And God will keep on loving us. But God isn't going to love us any more because we've made ourselves so wonderful. God will rejoice with us, but God isn't going to love us more, because God can't. There's no more to give once you've given everything. And so it's all gift. But as Paul says in 1 Corinthians 12–14, there's this funny thing about the gifts we're given— basically, we're given these gifts not for ourselves, but for other people. The church as the body of Christ lives by the interchange of gifts that this implies. The gifts I need have been given to you. The gifts that you need have been given to yet others. The gifts are given to us individually, but the use of them binds us together in community. And in everything, they reassure us of God's love for all.

The spiritual wealth of the community depends on our willingness to share our gifts. It's surprising how often we fail to do that. It may be through sheer selfishness, but often it's the fault of false modesty. We have a tendency to minimize our own gifts. "Oh, well, that was easy," we say; "that was nothing. Anybody could do that." Or we hanker after other people's gifts, which somehow seem more desirable: "Oh, gosh, if I could only do that! Well, maybe I'll try doing that, even though it's completely unnatural to me. If I could manage to do that, I'd feel like I'd really accomplished something." In our hankering after other people's gifts, we neglect our own. We don't notice that, by barging in where we really don't have much to share, we're merely getting in the way of someone who could do the job more easily and effectively. And we forget that the gifts we've been given are vital to the life of the community.

We need to take our gifts very seriously. Each of us has something of great value to share. We may not know, just yet, what it is. It may be something we don't prize very highly. Well, of course we don't—it comes easily to us because it's a gift. And we so much want to earn our way in this world; we so much want to put God in our debt. There's a part of us that greets the news of God's graciousness, God's love for us, by responding, "Well, this is all very well for you; but, I'm sorry, I have higher standards. I expect to earn my way!" Look at what you do well. Look at what you love. Look at what you are deeply drawn to. And take it seriously (not solemnly).

A Call to Community

Our lives are not defined only by gifts. There's also the matter of vocation, the idea that we are all called by God into a kind of partnership. Vocation doesn't mean what we often reduce it to—ordination. That's a very artificial narrowing of the whole concept. The seventeenth-century writer Jeremy Taylor was quite clear on this. Your vocation is your life, lived out in the way that you and God work out together, a way uniquely appropriate to who you are and also linking you to the world in which you live. The church and the gay and lesbian community both get into trouble when we neglect that truth, when we assume that everyone should be living out exactly the same pattern of life.

The lesbian and gay community, for example, sometimes battles about who is or isn't politically active enough. One group condemns another as spineless, and the other group complains that the first group is so in-your-face that it's alienating the whole world. Everybody's tempers get inflamed. What everyone seems to forget is that social change takes place through many agencies. People of differing vocations need one another. The activists give people at large a good fright or a wake-up call, and the people who are more moderate gain by that, because they can get a hearing that they weren't getting before. On the other hand, it usually takes the more moderate voices to help bring about a new consensus in the larger society. The activists can't do it alone because they work by alarming people and creating tensions; the moderates can't do it alone because they speak quietly enough that they can be ignored.

This is a pervasive reality of our lives. There's no single way to accomplish all that needs to be done. Anything of great human importance is complicated enough that it has to be attacked from many different angles. So we need to appreciate the variety of our gifts and our vocations. We need to learn how to appreciate the people who are doing what we can't do or aren't called to do. At the same time, we need to appreciate what we find ourselves being pulled into doing, whether by talent or by temperament or by some sense of responsibility that just won't go away.

Sometimes we discover our vocations reluctantly, but we know that's where we have to be. I had a conversation with a man, not long ago, who had been anointed by the media in his area as the person who would symbolize the reality of people who were gay and Christian. He is a fairly private sort of person and really didn't like becoming a public figure and having television cameras intrude on his birthday party and so forth. And yet, he had a sense that this is what he was called to be doing right now and that it was important enough that he had to put up with it. Whether you discover your vocation by finding that it's something you really want to do or just by knowing that this is what you're supposed to do right now, it is likely to stretch you. But even if it's uncomfortable at times, ultimately there is nothing more rewarding than sharing your gifts, in the ways you have been called to, with the rest of the community.

The Vocational Challenge of Being Gay

Living with the church will not be easy in our lifetimes. And I suppose if it ever becomes easy, we should get worried, because when it gets easy to live with the church, it probably means we're in a state of advanced idolatry and no longer capable of recognizing that the church is not God. We see plenty of this in American Christianity. People are outraged at the suggestion that there might be anything to Christianity that they haven't known since their early Sunday school years. They are incensed by the suggestion that God might have been moving on in the intervening time. Fundamentalists like to talk about the authority of the Bible, but it's very difficult actually to get them to read it with any purpose other than plugging the loopholes in their own systems. The idea that the Bible might contain some opportunity for new insight—even for a change of heart—is too threatening. I have a lot of sympathy with their plight, but, if they want to be in touch with God, they're going to have to go *through* the desert of uncertainty and disorientation rather than trying to take up permanent residence in it in fortified enclosures while growing steadily more and more desiccated in spirit.

Our goal isn't to become completely comfortable with the church. It's to learn how we can live with the church intelligently and faithfully, trusting God's initiatives toward us, God's encounters with us, God's continuing good will. We can accept that the church and religion in general are necessary things, but not always good things. We can recognize that, while we have some responsibilities toward our religious communities, we also have some responsibilities toward ourselves. In fact, if we don't take care of ourselves and see that we get the sustenance we need, pretty soon we won't have much to give. It's important to take our gifts seriously, and to follow the calling of God step by step, and to recognize that we don't have to do it all by ourselves. Other people have gifts that will sustain us; other people have vocations that will complement what we can do. That means that we can afford to shed the impossible burden of being God and making it all come out right. We can't really do that anyway. So why not give it up in advance?

If we can mature in this way, give up the simple binary oppositions, and recognize that human life is always going to be complex, we will reap spiritual benefit from our connection with the church. But as I said before, I suspect that the major traffic in our time has to go the other way: the church needs what gay and lesbian people have to offer, even more than we need what the church has to give us. And so, once we recognize the God we have encountered as the God of the gospel, then there's a vocation right there—to share with others the good news we've heard ourselves. We can count on having a set of gifts to make our vocations possible.

BILL: OUR PARTICULAR PRIESTHOOD

Being a Blessing to Ourselves and Others

Our experience of God, as gay and lesbian people, contains a blessing both for ourselves and for other people. It's at the heart of our particular priesthood. I'm thinking of the fundamental human priesthood here, the one that belongs to all humans. We cannot escape our priestly vocation. We can do it badly, but we cannot *not* do it at all. We would have to cut ourselves off from human society entirely in order not to do it at all, and we can't do that and still be human. So we live as priests and as people who need the help of other priests. We never get beyond the point of needing the priesthood of others, no matter how accomplished we get in our own priesthood.

Our specific priesthood isn't defined simply by the fact of our being gay or lesbian. That can't be a complete description of our priesthood, because it's not a complete description of us. Our priesthood emerges from our whole existence, our whole being, our temperament, our gifts, our weaknesses, our likes, our dislikes, the good things that have happened to us, the bad things that have happened to us, the moments when we've been close to God, the moments when we've felt there was no way to get to God. All of these things go into making up our priesthood, and any group of gay and lesbian people will be just as diverse as any group of specifically heterosexual people or any group of people in general. We are not defined by our sexuality alone. Nobody is.

Still, as gay and lesbian people, we do share the reality of being shaped by a minority sexual orientation, one that has been condemned and rejected and treated with a great measure of disgust and distress in our culture for a long time. So it's at least worth thinking what gifts that experience may bring to the priesthood that each of us exercises as a human being. I don't have any comprehensive list of those gifts. I'm not sure anyone's in a position to draw one up. But it should be helpful to suggest some areas that are worth looking at. The point is for all of us to be exploring our vocations as priests, not to provide a once-and-for-all, detailed formula of how lesbians or gay men "do" priesthood.

Forcing ourselves into such a formula would do us no more good than
trying to force ourselves into the heterosexual formula has. In the first
place, it won't work. In the second place, vocation is about the whole
person, not about stereotypes and categories, which can capture only
very little of who we are.

Being an Odd Sort of Minority

Belonging to a sexual minority, specifically the gay and lesbian sexual
minority, is radically different in one respect from being a member of,
say, a racial or ethnic minority. If you're a member of a racial or ethnic
minority, you were born into that minority and in most cases raised in
a family of that minority. You acquired your identity from childhood.
It was given to you by the culture. From the perspective of the majority culture, it may have been treated as something bad, but your own
community would have some sort of self-understanding that would
help you deal with that. As you grew up, you may have rejected parts of
this spiritual inheritance, but at least it was there and available to you.
Gay and lesbian people, by contrast, are usually born into heterosexual
families. There are a few exceptions, and some of us have met with
affirmation from our families despite our difference from them. But, in
one way or another, all of us have had to find ourselves, had to respond
to something within which told us that we were not quite the same as
the people we were living among. We have had to go out and find a
community and create families that had different characteristics. This
hasn't always meant leaving our natal families behind, but it does mean
that we have a dimension of experience that's unusual in our world.

All of us who are gay or lesbian have mixed identities. Heterosexuals,
by contrast, are apt to perceive themselves, I think, as just "standard
issue." It's a definition that doesn't tell you much about yourself,
because, after all, all people are that way, aren't they? The same quality
of being "standard issue" attends being Caucasian in our culture, or
being male. You're not forced to think about who you are, at least not
beyond the question of what distinguishes you as an individual. But
when a white male comes out, he discovers that there is this other element that has to be mixed in. This mixture of identities may be more
obvious to gay and lesbian people who belong to ethnic or racial
minorities. They combine a number of relatively clearcut and distinct
social identities. Perhaps, for an African American gay man, being
African American may be more of an issue in terms of the larger culture than his being gay. His being gay may be more of an issue within
the African American community. So there is a whole collection of
identities that we may belong to.

All this means that we're constantly crossing boundaries. At times it gets really wearing. But it's also a source, potentially, of great strength. Sometimes we refuse that strength. We refuse it by walling ourselves up inside little gay enclaves. I'm not saying that it's bad to have community venues that are predominantly lesbian and/or gay male. I'm saying that walling ourselves up inside them is a bad thing, an artificial limitation on ourselves, even a kind of giving in to the pressures from without. But if we do continue to participate in the larger human community, which most of us do in one way or another, we may very well find that we have an easier time moving back and forth between various minority communities and understanding the importance of different social identities than do people who have not had our particular experience.

If I were not a gay man I would know very little about belonging to minority communities: I'm overeducated, that's a kind of minority community; I'm an Episcopalian, and that's certainly a minority community in the United States. But those are not things that constantly impinge on my life in recognizable ways. Having come face to face with the reality of being a gay man, I understand a lot more of what people tell me about other kinds of minority experience. I can't *predict* what they will have to tell me. The experience of a person who belongs to an ethnic or racial minority is not the same as mine. But I have acquired ears to listen with. We have a very important ministry or priesthood we have that arises out of that reality. We are not people who can rest easily in a single identity. We know what it means to be defined *out*.

Being Sexual

Another element in our priesthood arises from the simple fact of our being labeled sexual beings, in contrast, again, to the heterosexual majority that thinks of itself as "standard issue," and therefore not as particularly sexual. For the heterosexual person, as such, sex is something you do, not something you are. Of course, we all wind up having to think about ourselves as sexual at various points in our lives. But heterosexual people can take that or leave it at any given moment, whereas our culture has made it a permanent part of our identity. One can resent that reality (Who wants to carry that whole rather uncertain bag for society at large?) or appreciate it. (As M. R. said once, it's sort of nice to be defined in terms of your desires in your late fifties.) But either way, it's there.

It's also, in its own way, a strength, an opportunity. It's an opportunity to delve deeper into a whole array of very difficult issues our culture is struggling with, issues involving sexuality, love, family, marriage, and singlehood, for example. These emerge in many forms, both in the

larger society and in the lesbian and gay community. There's the whole
conflict over gay unions and committed partnerships. Do we really
want those treated as marriage? Yes, in some ways. Legally, it would be
a great thing, because we would enjoy the rights to care for our partners in sickness and to share our property and to inherit, the sorts of
things that heterosexual people routinely enjoy. There are far too many
ugly stories about gay men with AIDS whose relatives would have nothing to do with them because of their illness, but seized the entire con-
tents of their homes after they died, including property that belonged
to their partners. Yes, legally it makes sense. But a lot of gay men look
at the institution of marriage as it currently exists and say, "Well, when
it works, it's great; but most of the time it doesn't work. Why would we
want to take on a heterosexual institution that's got its own problems?"

On the other hand, is there some understanding that emerges in gay
and lesbian partnerships that might, in fact, be beneficial to heterosexual marriage? I think probably so. It may well be easier for two men or
two women in our culture to work out what it means to be equals as
domestic partners than it is for a man and a woman, who have been
culturally defined in ways that contrast them with each other. It may
very well be that if the institution of marriage (the *sacrament* of marriage, in church terms) can be expanded to include gay and lesbian people, then it might be the institution itself that benefits most. We find
ourselves having to reflect a good deal on the way we relate to each
other, sexually and personally, since there is less determined beforehand.
Of course, that's not always a welcome thing—it's scary to be experiencing that kind of freedom—but it's also an opportunity for thinking
about things in new ways.

The tight link that Christianity has made between sexuality and marriage has to be looked at, too. The churches, by and large, have decided
to look the other way and not notice that that exclusive link no longer
holds with most younger heterosexual people. Even those that are most
rigid in theory are often surprisingly tolerant in practice. But it's hard
to think seriously about a subject you can't speak of. The experience of
many gay men is that sex is more than one thing. Sex may indeed be at
the heart of a committed lifelong partnership, but, under other circumstances, it may also be a way of expressing friendship. Sex may even
at times be a way, for some men, of simply participating in the reality
of gay community. These are things that some outsiders would quickly
label "promiscuity." Perhaps they are, but perhaps not. Again, you can't
really think about these things if you can't talk about them, if you
merely react negatively and refuse to listen to what such experience has
meant to those who have had it. Gay and lesbian people are, at this
point in our history, in a unique position of being able to ask fundamental questions about human sexuality.

One of the things about being gay or lesbian, after all, is that we eventually have to decide that the culture was wrong about at least one big part of what it was telling us about sex. That does not leave the rest of what our culture's been telling us untouched. Even if we decide to accept all the rest, it's our decision, not something inevitable. We have to start figuring out which parts of it we think are true, which parts of it actually seem to reflect the way sex works in human beings and human communities. That calls for some real reflection and some long, hard thinking. Some of us land pretty easily in relationships that are fully satisfying and don't find that we have to do much experimenting to sort out the sexual side of being gay. That's fine. But for a lot of us, it isn't that easy, and the process of experimentation doesn't always yield quick or obvious results.

All this is significant for a very large group of people who tend to be ignored by the church even when they're very much a part of it: people, both homosexual and heterosexual, who are single. A friend who moved to the East Coast recently, a single, heterosexual woman, tells about visiting a local church. There she was, by herself, no wedding ring—as obviously single as you can be nowadays—and the person who greeted her at the door told her how much she was going to like this church because it was a big family church and there were so many things for families to do. She had just had it with that sort of thing, and she said, "Well, you know, that's not really an attraction for me, since I'm single," and the greeter was dumbfounded. It hadn't occurred to him that a wonderful family church might not be the ideal choice for single people.

Family is "standard issue" in American culture. And therefore those who are comfortably ensconced in families aren't forced to reflect on what that means. The church has lots and lots of single people in it, and for the most part, the church serves them poorly. In particular the church has not wanted to deal with one very critical reality of single life today, namely that being single doesn't mean being nonsexual. This is not the world of the early or even middle of the century. In the beginning of this century, if you were single, chances are you were living with a parent or a married sister or brother. That had its own rewards, I'm sure. But that's not how singlehood operates now. Now we have a great many people who are single by choice or by happenstance—they've just never met anybody they truly wanted to settle down with—or because of the death of a partner or because of divorce. These are not people who are vowed to celibacy, nor should they be. They are not people are called to celibacy. (It's funny how the church tries to turn celibacy into a law, when Paul is perfectly clear in 1 Corinthians 7:36–38 that it's a gift, and not a law, and cannot be required as a law.) These are not people to whom it seems obvious that they can or should rule sexual relations entirely out of their lives. And the church is, for the most part, pretending that nothing has changed since 1918.

The reality of single life today is simply not being addressed in the churches. In many ways it may be easier for gay people to do the fundamental thinking here than it is for their heterosexual counterparts, if only because heterosexuality is standard issue. We have already made some space for self-discovery. Can we make use of it to offer insights to others? I'm not claiming that we have a monopoly on insight—just that this may be an area where our particular experience prepares us for a kind of priesthood to the larger community

Being Friends

Another thing that strikes me in my experience is that gay and lesbian people can often cross gender boundaries in a way that's difficult in purely heterosexual friendships. This happens in friendships between lesbians and gay men. It's also been a kind of truism, almost a stereotype, that gay men and straight women often form very close bonds. I know of a few cases of this happening between lesbians and straight males. Perhaps it's not as common; if not, I suspect it's the anxiety of straight males that makes it difficult. It can happen, though, and I suspect there would be similar benefits on both sides if there were more of it. It's possible for the two genders, opposed to each other as they have been in our culture, to get some actual communication going in situations where the absence of sexual attraction, at least on one side, simplifies things. Some things are just easier to deal with in a slightly simpler context.

Perhaps this also suggests that we may bring some special insight for people of our own gender. Lesbians have been very much engaged in the women's movement all along and have been in many cases powerful leaders of it. At times, people have almost identified lesbianism with the women's movement. Lesbians were able to conceive of women as independent beings in their own right, before many heterosexual women could. I don't believe the thinking and experience of gay men have been as centrally useful to heterosexual men. But our culture may yet find it helpful in developing models of manhood that do not depend on assuming that women are followers or that other men are always and only competitors. Those images of heterosexual masculinity have long since become destructive in our world.

The important thing on both sides is that we love people of our own gender. This love is erotic, and we become intensely aware of it because it's forbidden. We have to wrestle with it and try to figure it out and understand who we are. But even if it is erotic drive, it is not limited to genital expression; often it doesn't even seek genital expression. Love is much broader than that. Love can never be simply confined to the genitals. I suspect there is an erotic tinge in my friendships with straight men. It doesn't mean that I want to get them into bed. It does mean that I pay attention to them in ways that they may very well not be able to pay attention to each other. That's just how I'm focused. I don't think the present day is a particularly easy time for heterosexual men. They are still on top of the heap in terms of salaries and influence, but it's harder and harder to say who they are. That's an inherently unstable situation. It will benefit the whole of society if gay men can make use of their own experience of maleness and their ability to focus on men, discovering or creating ways of being male that will be an improvement over much of what we have inherited, with its emphasis on competition and its acceptance of violence.

Being Family

Another area where lesbian and gay experience potentially grounds an important element of our priesthood is the family. We have been pushed into discovering a sense of community that's larger and more generous than the nuclear families most of us grew up in. The idea of the nuclear family as the basic building block of society isn't really all that old in our culture. Back at the beginning of the century it was routine to have the maiden aunt or the bachelor uncle as part of the family, and maybe some grandparents, as well. A lot of labor-intensive domestic work was done in groups by women who belonged to the same household or by groups of neighbors. The relative isolation of the suburban housewife became possible only with the invention of "labor-saving" devices. The idea that the nuclear family had to stand on its own two feet was largely a product of the post-Word War II era, when it was conceived as a reward for returning veterans and (some would say) a way to sell goods and keep the economy afloat. I remember, from my childhood, when the women's magazine *McCall's* began calling itself "The Magazine of Togetherness." It was trying to position itself as the icon of this new concept of the self-contained, the self-enclosed nuclear family.

The shift proved, I think, to be not altogether healthy. It demanded much of family members and gave them really rather little support in the process. The man was the sole wage earner, totally responsible for the economic well-being of the family. The wife was confined to the domestic sphere without even as much housework as would have been the case in a previous era, and other women around her were confined to their houses in a similar way. Children had just two adult family members to relate to. Everyone else was secondary. It was not the richest environment.

It's still, however, the basic picture that we carry with us in the United States of how the family is supposed to work. It's what we use to judge everything else by, including our own current reality, when most families feel the need to have at least two adult wage earners and many children have to spend part of their day without adult supervision.

Some right-wing folk even claim that the post-War ideal represents biblical family values, which is a real joke. Biblical family values were focused on large polygamous households, where the children of different mothers competed with each other for the right of succession. Such households also included a lot of slaves and general hangers-on. That's how the model family worked in the biblical era. If you read the rules about sex and family in the Torah with care, you'll find that they're written with that type of family in mind. By the New Testament era, concurrent plural wives have largely disappeared in favor of a more serial kind of polygamy, but not much else had changed. There were just the glimmerings, among advanced thinkers, of an idea that husband and wife (who were often decades apart in age) might learn to become each other's friends and supporters.

The idea of making Jesus the patron of our mid-century family values is pretty funny, too. His mother and his brothers, on one occasion, came to collect him because they thought he was crazy. He refused to go out and see them and instead said to the people around him, "Who are my mother and my brothers and my sisters? . . . Whoever does the will of God is my brother and sister and mother" (Mark 3:21, 31–34). Early Christianity continued this pattern by substituting the church for the family of origin. That's why, in writings like First John, the Christians call each other "brother" and "sister" and "children." Well on down into the late Roman Empire, one of the things that pagans held against Christians was that they broke up families. St. Agnes, for instance, refused to marry the man her parents had chosen for her because he was a pagan and was martyred as a result. And St. Perpetua's father came to her in the prison with her baby son and said, "You can't go through with this martyrdom. Look, here's your child. You have to come back and take care of him." But she said, "No. I have a higher calling."

From Jesus onward, early Christianity was very disruptive of family life. The family was distrusted because of its tendency to absolutize itself. After all, it was the basic social unit in antiquity. You didn't count as an individual; you counted only through membership in a family, as parent, child, slave, freed person, client, or whatever. You counted in society only in terms of these roles. And the family's overarching concern was to preserve itself by reproduction, to amass greater wealth (or at least not lose any to other families), to increase in public reputation, and to make good connections through marriage. In other words, the family in and of itself had no particular spiritual concerns. The family existed for its own sake. And so Jesus called his disciples away from their families, and even after Jesus' time Christians continued to be disruptive of family life. Even after Christianity became legal, a really serious Christian might very well choose to run away to the desert and become a single person, a *monachos*, a monk, a hermit, or a member of a monastic community.

The modern nuclear family is in difficulty right now. The Christian response to that is not to say, "Oh, my God, we have to shore this up at all costs." Like early Christians, we should be open to meeting God, open to meeting our neighbor in God's presence, and God in our neighbor's presence, and see what comes of that. What will come of it, I hope, will be a larger and more generous kind of human family, which will include nuclear families, without idolizing them. Gay and lesbian people have a lot of experience in learning what such families might look like. We have achieved a surprising degree of stability and support in our families of choice, even though they may seldom be patterned on the nuclear family. That experience should be of use to others as our whole culture works to sort out how we can create family structures that will not just make demands on their members but also give them the support they need to lead rich and productive lives.

Being Alive in the Face of Death

Finally, one other area where the experience of gay and lesbian people in our times gives a unique slant to our priesthood: in the Western world, at least, we are the people who have had to acknowledge the reality of death in ways that the larger culture has largely managed to avoid. That's because of AIDS, of course; but I think it has enlarged our sensibilities so that we understand that death of any sort is something that needs to be dealt with in the context of family and friends, not isolated in antiseptic environments. We are the people who bore the brunt of discovering that death could still walk into the middle of the late-twentieth-century world, that modern science is not a cure-all, that death can claim the young as well as those who have had long and rich lives, and that death is a public issue and not just a private one. Death is a community thing as well as a personal thing. Out of that have come some extraordinary things—some extraordinary poetry, some extraordinary art, some extraordinary expressions of compassion.

One example is the Names Project Quilt. What a powerful expression of grief, of hope, of loss, and of expectation! Some of it's clumsily done, some very elegant, some easy to relate to, some really in-your-face. It's not morbid like the early nineteenth-century memorial tablets—the ones with the young woman leaning over the urn, the weeping willow hanging over her, and the soppy poem underneath. It doesn't wallow in death, but it acknowledges it as part of life. I think our whole culture will become healthier as we all learn to embrace death in that fashion, not to cut ourselves off from the awareness of it the way we have done for so long. For most of my life, death was something that was supposed to be hidden away—almost an embarrassment, a shameful thing, an acknowledgment of defeat. Gay and lesbian people have been helping to change that.

Being Priests

I'm not trying to describe the priesthood of every gay and lesbian person. There are gay men and lesbians whose priesthood turns on none of these things. None of us, after all, is defined simply by being gay or being lesbian. I'm just suggesting that these are some things that affect us as a community, some possible gifts, some things to think about. Sometimes our shared human priesthood functions through groups as well as through individuals. Perhaps these may be some of the things that we as a community have to share with the larger community of humanity, particularly in the church, but outside it as well.

I think our experience as Christians gives added dimension to what we can contribute. We don't, for example, see death as less real than anybody else. Christianity is not an easy way of accommodating oneself to loss by pretending that it doesn't really matter. But we do see even death as containing seeds of hope, because of the kind of God we believe in. I don't mean to say that resurrection simply cancels death and means that there is no problem. That would be facile and unconvincing. I mean rather that we have experienced the kind of God who has never abandoned us to our disasters and whom we cannot imagine abandoning us to the disaster of death. Not that we won't have to walk through the fire—we will. But we have believed in someone whose powers are not limited by the fire and who will not let us go.

Again, our religion actually brings us a rich tradition of reflection on family (ignored by the purveyors of the "biblical family values" silliness) that may have something to contribute to late-twentieth-century Western problems. We might conceivably find all sorts of riches in that tradition to bring to bear on the new situation, not only in the New Testament, but in the monastic tradition. Monastic vows, after all, are not radically different from vows of marriage. Yes, marriage is supposed to include sexual relations and monastic vows are supposed to exclude them. But they're both about creating new families in the same way that God created Israel out of the descendants of Jacob and the mixed multitude that went up with them out of Egypt, or the same way that God created the church out of Jews and Gentiles. God likes to take unrelated people and make new households out of them. There might be room for a lot of different configurations of family in our world, if we took more seriously this strange propensity God has for linking together people who don't "belong" together in advance.

This is an opportunity, as well, for us to reclaim and be enriched by the Christian doctrines of creation and incarnation. I remember the look of shock on the face of a longtime student of theology when it suddenly hit him that if Jesus was a genuine human being, and specifically a male, then Jesus must have had sexual reactions. He must have had erections. They never talked about that in Sunday school. What does it mean to think about a Jesus who was human in every sense, who is really enfleshed? For one thing, it means we have to take our own bodies more seriously as gifts of God. We affirm these doctrines of creation and incarnation in all our creeds. But having enshrined them in the creeds, we tend to ignore them in practice.

It's time to restore these central beliefs and benefit from them, even if it means a reversal of long-held assumptions. Christianity has mostly talked about the spirit being saved, with the body as a kind of appendix. Oh yes, you'll get your body back at the resurrection, but of course it won't have any of those inappropriate responses. This tradition, however old, really won't do. It's not biblical, and it's not orthodox. We are at the point of struggling toward genuine orthodoxy in that regard, and I suspect that, as we struggle toward it, we may help our secular brothers and sisters make sense of some of their experiences, too.

In this way, our Christian faith and our experience as gay and lesbian people join to create new ways of looking at common problems and possibilities. If our experience as gay men and lesbians gives us particular gifts for priesthood, that doesn't mean we're more priestly than anybody else. I've been ministered to by heterosexual people as well as by homosexual people, and I can't say that one group was better at it than the other. But it does mean that we have a certain responsibility to take our experience seriously, to see what our particular experience, whether as individuals or as community, brings to the enriching of our priesthood. Our experience is not something to be left behind as we perform our priestly service to the world. Quite the contrary, it is a gift God has given us to share.

M. R.: ICONS, PROPHETS, FIRE-DANCERS

Gay Vocation: Being Icons for Others

All we've explored so far are only first steps, the foundation stones of a reclaimed and revivified communal memory, an articulation of communal experience that points us to our deep identity as spiritual beings, members of the family.

It is only a beginning, however, a way of pointing to the spiritual commonality of the gay experience of coming out. It still says nothing of the purpose of that long and often painful process. Why were we summoned to the journey in the first place? Why were we called to be God's gay tribe, God's other people? What is it we bring with us, what might God have had in mind in giving us so separate and distinct a family likeness?

Obviously, we can only make some very tentative inroads into the question, tentative suggestions that may require many hearts and minds to flesh the insights out. As badly fractured as we are as individuals and people, we may never grasp the fullest understanding of what God envisioned as our gift to God's whole people. But we can look at what our being gay has given us as we now stand, and offer some insights into its value in the lives of others, gay or straight.

It is our very woundedness, the fractures that we carry as a separate people in a hostile and condemning world, that makes us pervious to God's Spirit, open to the shattering and healing life of God in Christ. Life has not given us security enough to rest in the cocoon of custom or inherited beliefs: we are more vulnerable, both to the worst the world can do to us and to the best that God can cause to happen in us. In a sense, we are the doorways through which God can enter a society, a church, grown deaf to God's good news. We are the fractured blocks that God can use to bring down the walls that we have built against God's sweeping winds, the walls that keep God's reign outside.

The Vocation of Being Gay

We must affirm that being gay is not an accident, an illness or a sin. It is a calling, as fully a vocation as any other, and God help the person or the church who turns a deaf ear to it.

What are we called to? What particular and fully gay vocation has God given us? In one sense it can be called a ministry of presence: no parish, family, church, or community is the same when self-affirming lesbians and gay men are part of it. But more specifically, it goes far beyond self-affirmation, to the acceptance of a radical and energizing ministry that will give meaning to our own lives, and will add immeasurably to the shared life of the whole.

We are called to be gay icons for one another and for every other man and woman in the world, windows through which God's working in the world is glimpsed and finally grasped. Specifically, we are naturally icons of the spiritual life for others, gay or otherwise. Our lives, our journeys, and our very natures gifted us for it.

What is it, then, that lesbians and gay men model for each other, and for other Christians: what are we the icons *of*? As individuals we may each have very different callings, very different qualities to model. But *as a community* we can model several very important things for one another and our straight sisters and brothers:

1. *The courage to be who God intended us to be.*
We live in a world that makes being oneself hideously costly; we are all more or less distorted by the time we reach adulthood. Tragic enough in human terms, of course, but how much more heartbreaking to the God who loved us into being and who yearns for us to be what God so lovingly intended us to be. In a world of this kind, every openly gay man and woman's life is a statement of enormous courage that can give hope to others: This is what it looks like to keep faith with God's gift of the self. This, in fact, is what real courage looks like: not the violent, exploitive images of adventure films. It is a courage that gay and straight alike can see mirrored in our lives. We are the natural icons who bear witness to its possibility.

2. *Vulnerability as freedom and spiritual strength.*
"Vulnerability is the doorway to freedom." Catch-phrase of the human potential movement that it is, this statement nevertheless expresses a considerable truth. Vulnerability is the chief risk of coming out, and also its greatest gift. Gay men and women are intimately acquainted with the frustrations, the fears, the crippling limits of a concealed and armored existence. Our freedom begins when we set aside the lies. This is not, of course, confined to God's gay people: the vulnerability of

Christ is our natural model, for God in Christ became absolutely vulnerable to us for our sake. This kind of vulnerability is the most powerful source of spiritual strength there is. Christ knew it. Gandhi knew it. Lesbian and gay Christians know it, too.

3. *The wholeness of being sexual/spiritual men and women.*
There is not a man or woman in our culture who is not, to some extent, a damaged and divided person. We are all the unfortunate victims of a culture whose religious side has taught us to repress, suspect, and downgrade our sexuality, while its commercial culture exaggerates, hypes, and exploits it. Gay and lesbian Christians are, of necessity, people who have had to struggle with their sexuality and its relationship to their spiritual lives. We may not always emerge as whole people, but we often come much further than our straight counterparts, who have not been forced to deal with it. We are icons of the wholeness that can be achieved when we can stand before God, fully spiritual beings, giving thanks that we are sexually gay.

4. *The willingness to love, and go on loving, no matter what the cost.*
This is the most profoundly spiritual gift of all. Make no mistake: this is the closest we can come to following the God whose willingness to love, and go on loving, stopped at no cost at all, not even crucifixion. We are a people defined by our loves. It is a wholly Christian message: Love is *always* costly; love is worth the cost. We are living icons of love's indestructibility, we who have loved despite two thousand years of suffering and terror. Nothing—not physical abuse or moral sanctions, not expulsion from our families or even the threat of death—has kept us from loving. This, if anything, is an icon we all need to contemplate from time to time, a living reminder that in the end, love can endure and outlast every other thing.

This is what gay men and women offer to one another and the church. Until that church can grant us gay saints of our own, we must be icons for one another, saints who bear one another's faith, one another's pride. And in the process, we become the windows through which others may, with God's help, see how awesome are the gifts that God grants ordinary human beings.

Gay Ministry, Gay Myth

These are the root tasks for gay spiritual ministry: the reclaiming of communal memory, the articulation of communal wisdom, and the affirmation of communal destiny—that is, our past, our present, and our future. These tasks cannot be achieved by merely taking models

from the straight tradition and appending our names to them. We are
God's gay tribe, called to traverse a different wilderness and called to
witness to a different kind of freedom. We must tell the stories, weave
the legends, paint the images that give it life and form. We are not
Abrahams or Sarahs yearning for the promised child. We are not the
conquering tribes who are commanded to go in and possess the land.
We will always be a small tribe, more or less a separate people, called to
live within the midst of others, yet with our own tribal languages and
customs. We need stories and myths that are the campfire wisdom we
pass on to others. We must shape them for ourselves.

In closing, let me offer one more story. This one story, plus that spare
and baffling parable called "Crossing the Sands," were all the survival
kit I was given to bring me through my own time in the desert. Call it
my dues, the thing I owe to our communal wisdom, that I pass it on. It
is the story of our pilgrimage and our identity.

Drying the Tears of God

This is the story of Hashad the Fool. Remember it.

> Hashad was a fool, there is no doubt about that! Who else but
> a fool would have done such a thing? But there, I'm getting
> ahead of the story. Let's begin at its beginning, please.
>
> He was a fool, this Hashad, and spent his days as only a
> fool would, standing in the marketplace and watching other
> people (sensible people!) do what sensible people ought to do:
> making rugs and selling pottery, or driving profitable bargains.
>
> One day, while he was standing around in this foolish
> manner, he saw a long line of people entering the marketplace.
> Men and women carrying odd-shaped bundles, camels loaded
> with rugs and bales, they did not stop to trade or haggle, but
> kept moving purposefully along. Intrigued and excited,
> Hashad fell into step beside a man who was striding along
> with a heavy bundle on his back and asked, "What's going on?
> Who are you? What is all this?" The man looked at him in con-
> temptuous surprise. "What is this? Why, any fool can tell what
> this is! It's a caravan."
>
> "Oh!" said Hashad." I've never seen a caravan before.
> Where are you going?"
>
> "What kind of fool are you?" demanded the man. "It's as
> plain as the nose on your face. We're on our way home from
> Istanbul with a load of rugs we've bought." And he trudged on,
> just as happy to get away from this ridiculous fool.

As Hashad was thinking about this, a woman driving a laden donkey along came abreast of him. "But this is wonderful!" exclaimed Hashad to the woman. "It must be wonderful to be on your way home from Istanbul with your load of rugs."

The woman glared at him. "What kind of fool are you?" she asked. "On our way home, indeed! Any fool can see what we're about. We're on our way to Baghdad with a load of fine embroidered clothes to trade."

"Oh!" exclaimed Hashad. "But that's even more exciting!" But by that time, the woman had stumped energetically on, and he found himself walking beside a very old man, who was murmuring to himself. "It must be very interesting, to be a trader on the road to Baghdad with a load of fine embroidered clothes to sell," he said to the old man.

"What's this about embroidered clothes? Don't be a fool, my boy! We're pilgrims, you know, pilgrims on our way to the shrine of the great saint Mevlana (peace be upon him!) in Konya." And he walked off, leaving Hashad staring after him in complete confusion.

By this time, all of the caravan had passed him by, except for one rather bored and dusty man who was leading a string of camels. "Please, sir, can't you tell me where you're going?" Hashad asked.

The camel man was impatient with him. "Look, they pay me to take care of the camels. It's not my job to know where we're going. If you want to know that, ask the Master of the Caravan. It's his job to know those things. I just take care of the camels, that's all."

"Well, then, where can I find the Master of the Caravan?" Hashad asked.

The man stared at him with astonishment. "You really *are* a fool! Any fool knows where the Master of the Caravan is. At the head of the caravan, of course! Up there somewhere." He waved his hand vaguely toward the front of the caravan.

Without so much as stopping to think twice about what he was doing, Hashad simply fell into step beside the camel man, determined to seek out the Master of the Caravan as soon as they had stopped for the night.

Now, why the poor fool thought he had to know these things, when far more sensible people didn't, who can say? But once his poor fool's brain got hold of an idea, there was no talking reason to him.

How Hashad tried to reach the Master of the Caravan! But he could never walk quite fast enough, or keep at it long enough, to reach the head of the caravan. A thousand times he forgot what he had set out to do because some new feature of the landscape caught his eye or because he got too interested listening to some fellow traveler's tale. Then he would remember his question and would struggle to make up for lost time.

Sometimes he caught a glimpse of a tall, imposing figure at the head of the caravan, only to lose sight of it again. Sometimes, when the wind was in the right direction, he caught the faintest sound of a great, resonant voice that must surely, surely be the Master of the Caravan. But each time, before he could press forward to be sure, he was jostled aside by an impatient traveler or distracted by some new and diverting thing he'd never seen before.

Anyone but a fool, of course, would have given up. But not Hashad. Someday, he was convinced, he would find the Master of the Caravan, and all his questions would be answered. He was a fool, and so he went on trying. Day followed day, and week followed week, and still Hashad trudged along, not a scrap wiser than he had been before.

One day, after many weeks of traveling through a very forbidding landscape, the travelers found themselves approaching a large, spacious-looking inn, just as the sun was going down. Travel-weary as they were, they rushed to it eagerly. Hot food, baths, and shelter from the weather: what more could they ask? When they bedded down that night, the tired travelers fell into a deep sleep.

But in the middle of the night Hashad awakened, aware that something was wrong, and found to his horror that the inn had caught fire. If he did not awaken the others and flee, they would all be trapped there to die. He leaped up and began to rouse the others. But some were so stupefied with sleep that they were angry at being awakened, and drove Hashad away, cursing at him. Others were so terrified that they stampeded in a panic, rushing straight into the fire itself. But a few kept their wits about them and began to search for a way out. Together they hunted until at last they found the gate.

But they found to their dismay that they could not reach it, for the fire stood between them and the gate! What could they do? They simply gave up, and lay down to wait for the end.

But he was a fool, this Hashad, too great a fool to understand that it was hopeless. And because he was a fool, and because he wanted to get out—wanted it so much he would try anything, anything at all!—he did the only thing left for him to do. He walked straight into the fire, and kept on walking, with his eyes upon the gate. The fool! And he would not turn back.

It was agonizing. Every nerve and cell screamed at him to give up, to go back, go back while he still could. But his fool's heart would not listen. On he pressed, straight through the heart of the fire, struggling toward the gate.

And then, just when he thought he could not endure another second, he fell forward—into cool, sweet air. He was free! He had walked through the fire!

Too stunned and in far too much pain to think, he lay gasping on the ground, unable to move. His hair was all but singed off, and his lungs were still aflame with pain, but he was alive, and he was free!

Then, as his senses returned, he noticed something. In front of him were two feet. He lifted his eyes slowly. Above the feet were two legs. And above the legs—the Master of the Caravan! He had found the Master of the Caravan at last.

Poor Hashad! After all his struggling to find the Master of the Caravan, he was so stunned that he couldn't even remember the question he had wanted to ask! It wouldn't have mattered if he had remembered, for before he could open his mouth, the Master of the Caravan looked at him with horror, and cried, "But where are the others, Hashad? How am I going to bring the others out?"

And Hashad's question died forever in his heart, because he saw that the Master of the Caravan's eyes were full of tears.

He was a fool, this Hashad, with a fool's heart, and the sight of those tears almost broke it. "Oh, please don't cry!" Hashad cried. "I know the way! I'll go!" And before his mind could catch up with his poor fool's heart, he had leaped back to his feet and turned to face the fire again.

So it is Hashad, finally, poor Hashad the Fool, the very least of all the least, who takes the Master of the Caravan by the hand and brings him through the heart of the fire, to find the others and to bring them out.

For this is what it means to be God's fool, and it is foolishness indeed, a madness no one undertakes *unless there is no other choice*. For it is this, you see, that Hashad the Fool was born for: to place his hand in the hand of God, and to pass and re-pass and re-pass through the fire, until the fire has lost its power to burn, and until he has learned to dance in the fire— to dry the tears of God.

This is the story of Hashad the Fool. Remember it.

At the Edge of the Sands

I dare not speak for tomorrow: I can only take the reality of our lives as they now stand. Someday, perhaps, these stories will no longer be the truth of gay experience. Someday, perhaps, gay children will grow up like others, and gay men and women will live lives no different from their straight brothers and sisters. Perhaps.

But in the meantime, there is Hashad the Fool, and a story which, far more than any other that I know, contains a truth about the meaning of gay pilgrimage. It may, in fact, be a completely human story, which will ring as true to others as it does to lesbians and gay men.

We are all this Hashad, this complete and utter fool, who begins the journey of his life without the slightest recognition of where he is bound. He does not even know, in fact, why he is traveling, or where he is likely to arrive. He cannot even find the one who knows the answers. He can only travel, in the dim hope that some day he will discover what the journey is about.

We must tell the story, we must pass it on, just as we live it out in our own lives.

If I have a word to add to the communal wisdom other lesbian and gay Christians may need to hold onto, it would be this: *We are God's fire-dancers, we the fools whose willingness to risk is the only way in which, somehow, God can reach back to bring the others out.* We do not have to know the answers, do not have to know where we are going, do not even have to know why out of all the world, God should have called us to be gay. We did not choose the fire, but our freedom may depend on walking through it.

We have only to remember our own journeys, only hold fast to the hand of God. With faith enough, with courage enough—and above all, with God's hand in ours—we may one day even learn to dance in the fire, as Hashad did.

We are God's fools, God's gay people, called to bear God company on this impossible and urgent journey: called to dry the tears of God.

God help us all.

NOTES

1. Throughout this book, the writer makes use of traditional Hanafiyya teaching stories and parables. Since this tradition is still maintained by oral teaching alone, and the original sources are conjectural, the translations, paraphrases, and retellings are her own.
2. See especially Carpenter's 1912 classics *Intermediate Sex: A Study of Some Transitional Types of Men and Women* (Kila, Mont.: Kessinger Publishing, 1999); and *The Drama of Love and Death: A Study of Human Evolution and Transfiguration* (London: M. Kennerly, 1912); Heard's *The Third Morality* (London: Cassell, 1937); *Pain, Sex and Time: A New Outlook on Evolution and the Future of Man* (New York: Harper Brothers, 1939); and the dense and often startling *The Five Ages of Man* (New York: Julian Press, 1963).
3. Christopher Fry, *The Firstborn: A Play in Three Acts* (London: Oxford University Press, 1950).
4. Fry, p. 123.
5. *The New English Bible* (London: Oxford University Press, 1970) (adapted).
6. John Boswell, *Christianity, Social Tolerance, and Homosexuality* (Chicago: University of Chicago Press, 1980), p. 16.

SELECTED BIBLIOGRAPHY

Abelove, Henry, Michèle Aina Barale, and David M. Halperin, eds. *The Lesbian and Gay Studies Reader.* New York: Routledge, 1993.

Aelred of Rievaulx. *Spiritual Friendship.* Translated by Maria Eugenia Baker. Kalamazoo, Michigan: Cistercian Publications, 1977.

Bawer, Bruce. *Stealing Jesus: How Fundamentalism Betrays Christianity.* New York: Crown Publishers, 1997.

Berkstresser, Charles Frank. *Christian Gay Men's Understanding of the Relationship Between Their Gayness and Their Spirituality.* M.A. thesis, Pacific School of Religion, 1991.

Bonneau, Normand, Barbara Bozak, André Guindon, Richard P. Hardy. *AIDS and Faith.* Ottawa: Novalis, 1993.

Borsch, Frederick H. *Sexuality and Christian Discipleship.* Cincinnati, Ohio: Forward Movement, 1993.

Boswell, John. *Christianity, Social Tolerance, and Homosexuality.* Chicago: University of Chicago, 1980.

_____. *Same-Sex Unions in Premodern Europe.* New York: Villard Books, 1994.

Bouldrey, Brian, ed. *Wrestling with the Angel: Faith and Religion in the Lives of Gay Men.* New York: Riverhead Books, 1995.

Boyd, Malcolm. *Are You Running with Me, Jesus?: An American Spiritual Classic Revisited.* Boston: Beacon Press, 1990.

_____. *Gay Priest: An Inner Journey.* New York: St. Martin's Press, 1987.

_____. *Half Laughing / Half Crying.* New York: St. Martin's Press, 1988.

_____. *Take Off the Masks.* San Francisco: Harper Collins, 1993.

Boyd, Malcolm, and Nancy L. Wilson, eds. *Amazing Grace: Stories of Lesbian and Gay Faith.* Freedom, California: Crossings Press, 1991.

Bronski, Michael. *Culture Clash: The Making of Gay Sensibility.* Boston: South End, 1984.

Brown, Peter. *The Body and Society: Men, Women and Sexual Renunciation in Early Christianity.* New York: Columbia University Press, 1988.

Butler, Judith. *Gender Trouble: Feminism and the Subversion of Identity.* New York: Routledge, 1990.

Carpenter, Edward. *The Drama of Love and Death: A Study of Human Evolution and Transfiguration.* London: M. Kennerly, 1912.

_____. *Intermediate Sex: A Study of Some Transitional Types of Men and Women* (1912). Kila, Montana: Kessinger Publishing, 1999.

Cherry, Kittredge and Zalmon Sherwood, eds. *Equal Rites: Lesbian and Gay Worship, Ceremonies, and Celebrations.* Louisville: Westminster/ John Knox, 1995.

Clark, Elizabeth A. *Jerome, Chrysostom, and Friends: Essays and Translations*. New York: Mellen Press, 1979.

Clark, J. Michael. *A Defiant Celebration: Theological Ethics and Gay Sexuality*. Garland, Texas: Tangelwüld Press, 1990.

_____. *A Lavender Cosmic Pilgrim: Further Ruminations on Gay Spirituality, Theology, and Sexuality*. Garland, Texas: Tangelwüld Press, 1990.

_____. *Diary of a Southern Queen: An HIV+ Vision Quest*. Dallas: Monument Press, 1990.

_____. *Gay Being, Divine Presence: Essays in Gay Spirituality*. Garland, Texas: Tangelwüld Press, 1987.

_____. *Theologizing Gay: Fragments of Liberation Activity*. Oak Cliff, Texas: Minuteman Press, 1991.

Cleaver, Richard. *Know My Name: A Gay Liberation Theology*. Louisville: Westminster John Knox, 1995.

Comstock, Gary. *Gay Theology without Apology*. Cleveland, Ohio: Pilgrim Press, 1993.

Coote, Stephen, ed. *The Penguin Book of Homosexual Verse*. Penguin Books: Harmondsworth: Middlesex, England, 1983.

Crew, Louie, ed. *A Book of Revelations: Lesbian and Gay Episcopalians Tell Their Own Stories*. Washington, D.C.: Integrity, 1991.

Cromey, Robert Warren. *In God's Image*. San Francisco: Alamo Square, 1991.

Cruikshank, Margaret. *The Gay and Lesbian Liberation Movement*. New York: Routledge, 1992.

Curb, Rosemary and Nancy Manahan, eds. *Lesbian Nuns: Breaking Silence*. Tallahassee, Florida: Naiad Press, 1985.

De Lauretis, Teresa. *The Practice of Love: Lesbian Sexuality and Perverse Desire*. Bloomington: Indiana University Press, 1994.

Denman, Rose Mary. *Let My People In: A Lesbian Minister Tells of Her Struggles to Live Openly and Maintain Her Ministry*. New York: Morrow, 1990.

Duberman, Martin Bauml, Martha Vicinus, and George Chauncey Jr., eds. *Hidden from History: Reclaiming the Gay and Lesbian Past*. New York: New American Library, 1989.

Fortunato, John E. *AIDS: The Spiritual Dilemma*. San Francisco: Harper & Row, 1987.

_____. *Embracing the Exile*. New York: Harper Collins, 1982.

Foucault, Michel. *The History of Sexuality*. Translated by Robert Hurley. Vol. 1. An Introduction. New York: Random House, Vintage, 1980.

Fry, Christopher. *The Firstborn: A Play in Three Acts*. London: Oxford University Press, 1950.

Garber, Linda. *Lesbian Sources: A Bibliography of Periodical Articles, 1970–1990*. New York: Garland, 1993.

Gilson, Anne Bathurst. *Eros Breaking Free: Interpreting Sexual Theo-Ethics.* Cleveland, Ohio: Pilgrim Press, 1995.

Glaser, Chris. *Come Home! Reclaiming Spirituality and Community as Gay Men and Lesbians.* New York: Harper Collins, 1990.

_____. *Coming Out to God: Prayers for Lesbians and Gay Men, Their Families and Friends.* Louisville: Westminster/John Knox, 1991.

_____. *Uncommon Calling: A Gay Man's Struggle to Serve the Church.* New York: Harper Collins, 1987.

Goss, Robert. *Jesus Acted Up: A Gay and Lesbian Manifesto.* San Francisco: Harper, 1993.

Grahn, Judy. *Another Mother Tongue: Gay Words, Gay Worlds.* Boston: Beacon, 1985.

_____. *She Who.* Oakland, California: Diana Press, 1977.

Gramick, Jeannine and Pat Furey, eds. *The Vatican and Homosexuality: Reactions to the "Letter to the Bishops of the Catholic Church on the Pastoral Care of Homosexual Persons."* New York: Crossroad, 1988.

Gross, Larry P. *Contested Closets: The Politics and Ethics of Outing.* Minneapolis: University of Minnesota, 1993.

Guindon, André. *The Sexual Creators: An Ethical Proposal for Concerned Christians.* Lanham, Maryland: University Press of America, 1986.

_____. *The Sexual Language: An Essay in Moral Theology.* Toronto: University of Ottawa Press, 1977.

Hefling, Charles, ed. *Ourselves, Our Souls and Bodies: Sexuality and the Household of God.* Cambridge, Massachusetts: Cowley, 1996.

Heard, Gerald. *Pain, Sex and Time: A New Outlook on Evolution and the Future of Man.* New York: Harper Brothers, 1939.

_____. *The Five Ages of Man.* New York: Julian Press, 1963.

_____. *The Third Morality.* London: Cassell, 1937.

Heyward, Carter. *Coming Out and Relational Empowerment: A Lesbian Feminist Theological Perspective.* Wellesley, Massachusetts: Stone Center, 1989.

_____. *Speaking of Christ: A Lesbian Feminist Voice.* Edited by Ellen C. Davis. New York: Pilgrim Press, 1989.

_____. *Staying Power: Reflections on Gender, Justice, and Compassion.* Cleveland: Pilgrim Press, 1995.

_____. *Touching Our Strength: The Erotic as Power and the Love of God.* San Francisco: Harper & Row, 1989.

Heyward, Carter and Sue Phillips, eds. *No Easy Peace: Liberating Anglicanism.* Lanham, Maryland: University Press of America, 1992.

Hocquenghem, Guy. *Homosexual Desire.* Durham, North Carolina: Duke University Press, 1993.

Holtz, Raymond C. *Listen to the Stories: Gay and Lesbian Catholics Talk about Their Lives and the Church.* New York: Garland, 1991.

Hunt, Mary E. *Fierce Tenderness: A Feminist Theology of Friendship.* New York: Crossroad, 1991.

Kushner, Tony. *Angels in America. Part I: Millennium Approaches.* New York: Theatre Communications Group, 1993.

_____. *Angels in America. Part II: Perestroika.* New York: Theatre Communications Group, 1993.

Lanphear, Roger G. *Gay Spirituality: Experiences in Self-Realization for Gay Men, Lesbians, and Enlightened Heterosexuals.* San Diego, California: Unified Publications, 1990.

Long, Ronald E. *AIDS, God, and Faith: Continuing the Dialogue on Constructing Gay Theology.* Las Colinas, Texas: Monument Press, 1992.

Mass, Lawrence. *Dialogues of the Sexual Revolution.* New York: Haworth Press, 1990.

McNeil, John. *Freedom, Glorious Freedom: The Spiritual Journey to the Fullness of Life for Gays, Lesbians, and Everybody Else.* Boston: Beacon, 1995.

_____. *Taking a Chance on God.* Boston: Beacon, 1988.

_____. *The Church and the Homosexual (revised edition).* Boston: Beacon, 1988.

Mohr, Richard D. *Gay Ideas: Outing and Other Controversies.* Boston: Beacon Press, 1992.

Mollenkott, Virginia Ramey. *Sensuous Spirituality: Out from Fundamentalism.* New York: Crossroad, 1992.

Nestle, Joan and John Preston. *Sister and Brother: Lesbians and Gay Men Write About Their Lives Together.* San Francisco: Harper Collins, 1994.

Nugent, Robert and Jeannine Gramick. *Building Bridges: Gay and Lesbian Reality and the Catholic Church.* Mystic, Connecticut: Twenty-Third Publications, 1992.

O'Neill, Craig and Cathleen Ritter. *Coming Out Within.* New York: Harper Collins, 1992.

Presbyterian Church (U.S.A.). *Presbyterians and Human Sexuality.* Louisville, Kentucky: Presbyterian Church (U.S.A.), 1991.

Riordan, Michael. *Out Our Way: Gay and Lesbian Life in the Country.* Toronto: Between the Lines, 1996.

Ritley, M. R. *God's Gay Tribe: Laying the Foundations of Communal Memory.* New Haven, Connecticut: Beloved Disciple Press, 1994.

_____. *Speaking for Ourselves.* D. Min. thesis, Church Divinity School of the Pacific, 2000.

Seaburg, Carl. *Inventing a Ministry: Four Reflections on the Life of a Colleague, Charles Vickery.* Boston: Minn Lectureship Committee, 1992.

Sedgwick, Eve Kosofsky. *Between Men: English Literature and Male Homosexual Desire.* New York: Columbia University Press, 1985.

_____. *Tendencies.* Durham, North Carolina: Duke University Press, 1993.

Spahr, Jane Adams. *Approaches to the Spirituality of Lesbian Women: Implications for Ministry.* D. Min. thesis, San Francisco Theological Seminary, 1987.

Stuart, Elizabeth, ed. *Daring to Speak Love's Name: A Gay and Lesbian Prayer Book.* London: Hamish Hamilton, 1992.

Thompson, Mark. *Gay Soul: Finding the Heart of Gay Spirit and Nature.* New York: Harper Collins, 1994.

————. *Gay Spirit: Myth and Meaning.* New York: St. Martin's, 1987.

Vickerman, Sue. *Christianity and Homosexuality: A Resource for Students.* London: Lesbian and Gay Christian Movement, 1992.

Warner, Michael, ed. *Fear of a Queer Planet: Queer Politics and Social Theory.* Minneapolis: University of Minnesota Press, 1993.

White, Mel. *Stranger at the Gate: To Be Gay and Christian in America.* New York: Simon & Schuster, 1994.

Wolf, James G., ed. *Gay Priests.* San Francisco: Harper & Row, 1989.

Zanotti, Barbara, ed. *A Faith of One's Own: Explorations by Catholic Lesbians.* Trumansburg, New York: Crossing Press, 1986.